JOHN MILTON

JOHN MILTON

❧ A Sketch of His Life and Writings ❧

by Douglas Bush

COLLIER BOOKS, *NEW YORK*

FIRST COLLIER BOOKS EDITION 1967

Library of Congress catalog card number: 64-7786

John Milton was originally published in a hardcover edition by The Macmillan Company.

The Macmillan Company, New York
Collier-Macmillan Canada Ltd., Toronto, Ontario

Printed in the United States of America

◄(◄(◄(◄(PREFACE   )►)►)►)►

This small book is not addressed to Miltonic specialists. It is, on its very limited scale, a biographical and critical introduction for those who are reading Milton seriously for the first time or have felt the happy impulse to reread him. I have drawn gratefully upon countless books and articles, but a sketch of this kind cannot be weighted down with what Milton called a "horse-load of citations." Quotations from his and other early writings are modernized in spelling and punctuation, except for observing the elisions that attest the poet's concern with the number of syllables in a line. Translations from Milton's Latin, unless a reference is given, are my own.

For precise information about the performance at the Barberini palace that Milton attended, I am indebted both to *John Milton, Englishman* and to a full private account from that book's author, Dr. James Holly Hanford— to whom all modern students of Milton have owed so much.

D.B.

❤❤❤❤❤ CONTENTS ❤❤❤❤❤

CONTENTS

PART FOUR

The Restoration: 1660–1674

The last dozen years have seen more books, essays, and articles on Milton, especially on *Paradise Lost*, than ever appeared before in the same stretch of time, many more than any English writer except Shakespeare has evoked. The fact is an external reminder that Milton's poetry is very much alive, that both his ideas and his art have been studied and illuminated in increasing depth, and that he remains, more securely than ever, the second of English poets, the greatest classical artist of the modern world in any language.

On the other hand, the literati who mold common opinion have not for decades granted Milton a place in the canon of poets who minister to our needs and should receive active homage. General literary criticism has been sparse in its references, and these seldom reflect interest, knowledge, or understanding. This conventional attitude seems to be based chiefly on three things: the notion of Milton's personal character as proud, harsh, and un-charitable; the sort of religion supposedly presented in *Paradise Lost* and *Paradise Regained*; and the nature of Milton's art, which is too remote from modern poetry to be useful for poets or attractive to readers. The first of these charges—which is of a kind that is rarely allowed to affect our response to other authors—does not appar-ently need to be supported by evidence; repetition, by people of unfailing humility and charity, is enough. In the history of literature, however, there can be few writers whose personal records do not yield more and darker blots than the total reckoning that can be compiled against Milton; indeed it may be suspected that most of the personal prejudice boils down to resentment of his earnest religious and moral uprightness. The religious quality of the epics will be discussed in later pages; it may be thought more authentic and satisfying than the results of our diligent search for "Christ figures" and images of the Fall in odd places. The third point has more validity, of a kind, since it is a commonplace that in our world neither writers nor readers have eyes and ears receptive to heroic vision and heroic utterance. But, however restricted poets' sympathies may or must be, readers enjoy a more catholic freedom—unless their sensibility has been stunted by the normal contemporary limitation of poetry to wry little footnotes on life. If this paragraph will serve to register a somewhat outdated indifference or antipathy, we may henceforth be concerned with a positive view of a great man and one of the world's greatest poets.

Milton may be called the most heroic figure in English poetry, not merely because he composed the great English epic but because he was a personality of heroic stature whose experience, as we follow it, becomes itself a heroic poem or drama, and a very moving one.

Our personal acquaintance begins at the beginning of Milton's second year at Cambridge. In and between the lines of his academic speeches and private letters and his early Latin and English poems we get a picture of a strong, sensitive, and morally fastidious young man who rises from some initial unpopularity to the enjoyment of friendly esteem; an ardent, liberal humanist who rebels against the scholastic curriculum and has a large and thrilling vision of a new era in England and the world that he may help to inaugurate; a scholarly, religious, and extremely sensuous poet who is devotedly intent on learning his craft. Even while at Cambridge Milton moved, in both Latin and English verse, from apprenticeship to mastery.

Up through *Comus,* Milton's early poems embodied a sheltered and serene but glowing idealism, religious or courtly or both. The transition from songs of innocence to songs of experience came with the reverberating inner conflicts of *Lycidas.* After his Italian tour, when, following the natural course of a Renaissance poet's ambition, Milton was ready to embark on an epic, his sense of religious and civic duty compelled him to abandon poetry for pamphleteering in the cause of liberty. From attacks on prelacy Milton went on to deal with divorce, education, freedom of the press, the right of the people to depose and execute King Charles. Becoming Secretary for Foreign Tongues to the Council of State, Milton wrote, for a European audience, two large Latin defenses of the regicides and the Commonwealth. The first of these cost him, at the age of forty-three, what remained of his failing eyesight. When the prolonged chaos that followed Cromwell's death was leading clearly to the Restoration, Milton was bold enough to publish, and to augment and republish, a last plea for a republic. As a notorious champion of the Commonwealth he was in serious danger of falling a victim, with others, to government reprisals (and he was held in custody for a time), but his life was spared.

How deep and lasting a wound Milton suffered from the Restoration we can imagine if we think of the unbounded optimism that had flamed through his early pamphlets; though by no means the first of the idealist's disillusionments, this was by far the heaviest. Instead of the holy community, the establishment of Christ's kingdom on earth, England had Charles II, and Milton was "Eyeless in Gaza at the mill with slaves." He might have

lapsed into sullen defeatism—and a cloud of realistic dis-
enchantment does hang over his last three works—yet his
religious faith was rather purified than defeated. He
never lost his vision of perfection, though its content
changed. In early poems, from some Latin elegies and the
Nativity to *Lycidas*, it had been quite literally a glimpse
of heaven; in the pamphlets the vision was translated
into a concrete, militant, revolutionary creed to be
realized here and now. But in *Paradise Lost* fulfillment
of that dream is to come only after the day of judgment;
in this and the two last works Milton takes his stand on
the impregnable ledge of rock that remains, his faith in
God and the individual soul, in love and humility, freedom and discipline.

The briefest outline of Milton's career attests his integrity and strength, the earnest commitment of both his
intellect and his conscience to great issues, public and
private. Without such experience and such commitment
he would not be the poet he is. And in no poet have
religious and political, intellectual and aesthetic experience and sensibility been more completely unified.

As for Milton the artist, criticism has got far beyond
the notion that he was a grandiose but simple-minded
rhetorician who splashed about with a big brush, and
that for subtle complexity we must go to Dante or Shakespeare or Donne. That notion, which gained currency in
some quarters a generation ago, grew partly out of low
esteem for "classical" art, in both the specific and the
timeless sense of the word. Anyone who would throw out
Milton must throw out the Greek and Roman poets too.
Whatever may be said about Milton and baroque, A. E.
Housman's old-fashioned tribute remains true: "The
dignity, the sanity, the unfaltering elevation of style, the
just subordination of detail, the due adaptation of means
to ends, the high respect of the craftsman for his craft
and for himself, which ennoble Virgil and the great

Greeks, are all to be found in Milton, and nowhere else in English literature are they all to be found."* Recent criticism has shown that both the organization and the texture of Milton's poetry are very subtle indeed, though the smooth surface is deceptive; we are not commonly inclined to recognize depth, complexity, and intensity unless these qualities are manifested in some erratic straining and disorder. But while Milton's highly sophisticated art can be most fully appreciated by those who know Greek and Latin poetry, he is more accessible to any intelligent and educated reader than a multitude of less learned and more fashionable poets.

Milton the artist, like Milton the thinker, was always developing. His early Spenserianism was soon fused with clear-cut Jonsonian urbanity. In *Lycidas* and the occasional sonnets emerged elements of the grand style which received full orchestration in *Paradise Lost*. There followed the "prosaic" plainness of *Paradise Regained* and the massive ruggedness of *Samson Agonistes*. In all these phases, except in a few of his earliest poems, Milton was writing in the classical tradition, although, like all great artists of masterful originality, he re-created every genre he touched; at the same time he re-created poetic language and rhythm. His evolution from youth to age might be roughly charted by his allusions to Orpheus, the archetypal poet. There is first the serene lyricism of *L'Allegro*, in praise of joyous music:

> That Orpheus' self may heave his head
> From golden slumber on a bed
> Of heaped Elysian flow'rs, and hear
> Such strains as would have won the ear
> Of Pluto, to have quite set free
> His half-regained Eurydice.

* *Introductory Lecture . . . in University College, London, October 3, 1892*. New York: The Macmillan Company; Cambridge: At the University Press, 1937.

To pass by the less happy reference in *Il Penseroso*, there are the harshly resonant and deeply significant lines in *Lycidas*:

> What could the Muse herself that Orpheus bore,
> The Muse herself for her enchanting son
> Whom universal nature did lament,
> When by the rout that made the hideous roar
> His gory visage down the stream was sent,
> Down the swift Hebrus to the Lesbian shore?

In the invocation to Light, when Milton moves from hell to heaven, he recalls the difficult ascent of Orpheus and Aeneas from the underworld, and the difference between pagan poetry and his own sacred theme and between his physical blindness and his inward light:

> Thee I revisit now with bolder wing,
> Escaped the Stygian pool, though long detained
> In that obscure sojourn, while in my flight
> Through utter and through middle darkness borne
> With other notes than to th' Orphean lyre
> I sung of Chaos and eternal Night,
> Taught by the Heav'nly Muse to venture down
> The dark descent, and up to reascend,
> Though hard and rare. Thee I revisit safe,
> And feel thy sovran vital lamp; but thou
> Revisit'st not these eyes, that roll in vain
> To find thy piercing ray, and find no dawn;
> So thick a drop serene* hath quenched their orbs,
> Or dim suffusion veiled.

Finally, when Milton is halfway through *Paradise Lost*, in a time when the Restoration has crushed all his dreams of a new Reformation, when he is fallen on evil days, in darkness, and with dangers compassed round, and solitude, the wicked world is identified with the frenzied Bacchic throng that had done Orpheus to death:

* A translation of the medical term *gutta serena*.

Still govern thou my song,
Urania, and fit audience find, though few.
But drive far off the barbarous dissonance
Of Bacchus and his revelers, the race
Of that wild rout that tore the Thracian bard
In Rhodope, where woods and rocks had ears
To rapture, till the savage clamor drowned
Both harp and voice; nor could the Muse defend
Her son. So fail not thou who thee implores;
For thou art heav'nly, she an empty dream.

PART ONE

Early Life
and Writings

1608–1632

1

St. Paul's School and Cambridge

MILTON WAS BORN in London on December 9, 1608, at his father's house and place of business in Bread Street, Cheapside, within the old mile-square City where the well-to-do lived. At this time London, with a population of well over 200,000 (nearly doubled by 1660), was one city, Westminster another; the area between and around these centers was made up of suburbs, isolated villages, and open fields. The chief thoroughfare was the "silver-streaming Thames" which Spenser—ignoring the raucous army of watermen whose boats were the first taxicabs—had adjured to "run softly, till I end my song." Spenser, driven from Ireland by another rising, had died in London in 1599; in 1608 Shakespeare was still living there, *The Winter's Tale* and *The Tempest* not yet written; Ben Jonson had done some of his great plays and launched the series of masques which Inigo Jones lavishly produced for the delectation of the court; Donne, with his wife and multiplying family, was in his difficult middle period and had perhaps just written *Biathanatos*, his defense of suicide; and several groups of scholars, Lancelot Andrewes and others, were working, in London, Oxford, and Cambridge, on what was to be the King James Bible. The king had been reigning nearly six years and had not yet grievously disappointed the high hopes that had welcomed his accession. But parliament had had cause to be uneasy; James's early declaration of Stuart policy, "No bishop, no king," had been ominous for the growing body of Puritans; and his pacific intentions toward Roman Catholics had been upset by the exposure of the Gunpowder Plot (November 5, 1605), a deliverance which has been annually celebrated down to our own day. To such celebrations at Cambridge Milton was to contribute a short Latin "epic" and some epigrams.

Religious nonconformity was one portion of the poet's family inheritance. According to early biographers, his Oxfordshire grandfather had in Elizabeth's reign held out as a Roman Catholic recusant and disinherited his son John, the poet's father, for turning Protestant. That son—who was said by John Aubrey to have attended Christ Church, Oxford (as a chorister or student or both?)—went to London and became a scrivener, that is, a notary and conveyancer. As he advanced in this humble branch of the law he took on the additional and profitable business of moneylending and in time amassed a comfortable fortune. He had therefore the means and, as the poet's grateful tributes testify, the active desire to provide his gifted elder son with the best available education and, after that, with years of leisure and foreign travel. Another kind of inheritance was important too. John Milton senior was a composer of some repute even in the golden age of English music before and after 1600. While he was not one of the major galaxy that included such men as William Byrd, John Wilbye, John Dowland, Thomas Morley, Thomas Weelkes, and Orlando Gibbons, he was good enough to be represented in Morley's anthology of madrigals, *The Triumphs of Oriana* (1601), and Thomas Ravenscroft's Psalter of 1621. Thus the poet grew up in a musical atmosphere, and his own continued devotion to music is attested by

the early biographers and by his many literal and symbolic allusions in prose and verse, allusions generally
marked by a special glow of language and feeling.

In this age mothers—unless they were socially prominent or temperamentally masterful, like Magdalen
Herbert, who was both—were wont to be inconspicu-
ously busy, competent, pious, and prolific. Of his mother
—who died in 1637—Milton said only that she was an
excellent woman who was held in high esteem for her
charities. The younger son, Christopher, after a short
stay at his brother's Cambridge college, became a bar-
rister; though he later took the royalist side, the two
remained on good terms. Milton's older sister Anne
married in 1623; her sons, Edward and John Phillips,
were to be their uncle's first pupils when he commenced
teaching, and Edward was to write one of the first biographies.

In 1618, when Milton was ten, the father had his son's
portrait painted (the portrait is now in the Pierpont
Morgan Library in New York). The handsome, auburn-
haired little boy, in a rich doublet and wide lace collar,
looks out with grave, thoughtful eyes. Perhaps as early
as 1615–1616 he had entered St. Paul's School, John
Colet's famous foundation, now a century old. The headmaster, Alexander Gill, was one of the many distinguished teachers of the age; he showed capacities of one
kind in his book on the English language, *Logonomia
Anglica* (1619), of another in his *Sacred Philosophy of
the Holy Scripture* (1635), a rational approach to Christian theology. Both lines of interest would have been
congenial to the older Milton, and the former at least
would have affected Gill's teaching. The boy seems to
have enjoyed the atmosphere and work of the school and
to have had it in mind as a criterion when he later re-
acted against the Cambridge curriculum and later still
when he wrote *Of Education*. Studies were almost

entirely classical; St. Paul's, like some other schools, included Hebrew in the last year. The prime object was complete mastery of Latin as a second native language. Latin was a practical, professional necessity, the international medium, the key to nearly all ancient and modern knowledge; the study of Greek was secondary, though not unsubstantial. Classical Latin and Greek of course embraced history, oratory, philosophy, poetry, and drama, and, along with the literature, intensive study of rhetoric and composition, especially in Latin. The general program had come down in unbroken continuity from the schools of the Roman empire, with Christian additions (a point on which Colet had been emphatic). The Renaissance had enlarged the classical corpus and historical and literary learning, and had provided modern textbooks of models and methods for composition, including useful phrase-books for young versifiers. Three short themes, one in prose and two in verse, have survived from Milton's schooldays; these were elaborations of a standard maxim on the advantages of early rising—advantages not always apparent to boys, though Milton, like many other men, kept up the habit throughout his life.

In his *Second Defence of the English People* (1654), replying to the charge that his blindness was a divine punishment, Milton said (in Latin):

My father destined me from childhood to the study of humane letters, and I took to those studies with such ardor that, from the time I was twelve, I hardly ever gave up reading for bed until midnight. This was the first cause of injury to my eyes, which were naturally weak, and I suffered from many headaches.

John Aubrey's similar report has the further detail that "his father ordered the maid to sit up for him." Milton himself—to continue the personal passage just quoted—said that since these handicaps did not check my eagerness to learn, my father, in addition to the regular schoolwork, saw to it that I was daily taught by other masters at home. After I had been thus instructed in the various languages, and had got no small insight into the charms of philosophy, my father sent me to Cambridge. . . .

We know one of these private tutors, the Scottish Thomas Young, who taught Milton in 1618–1620 and during 1620–1628 was in Hamburg as chaplain to the English merchants there. In the later 1620's Milton addressed to Young an epistle in verse and two letters in prose, all in Latin, and all carrying warm affection and respect. In the poem Milton seems to say, with grateful remembrance, that it was Young who introduced him to Latin poetry. From this piece and especially from the later Latin poem *To His Father*, it appears that private tutoring supplemented Milton's schoolwork in the classics and added French, Italian, natural science, perhaps also geography and music.

Two friendships which began in Milton's schooldays were of unequal importance. One mainly literary friend was the younger Alexander Gill, the headmaster's son and assistant and Milton's senior by a decade. He got into trouble in 1628 for some spoken and written gibes at King James, King Charles, and the Duke of Buckingham. In 1632 he published a volume of Latin poems. The two young men evidently sent verses to each other, and Milton in his Latin poems may have echoed some of Gill's. Milton had far closer bonds with Charles Diodati (1609–1638), the grandson of an Italian Protestant of Lucca who had gone into exile on account of his religion, and the son of a prominent physician who had married an Englishwoman. Charles entered St. Paul's probably in 1617 or 1618, when his father was practicing in London and living, like the Miltons, near the school. He went up to Oxford in 1623 and received his B.A. degree in 1625;

in 1624 he had a Latin poem in a volume of tributes to the deceased historian, William Camden. Two letters in Greek from Diodati to Milton survive, and Milton's first Latin elegy may be a reply to the second. Diodati was the one friend to whom Milton poured out his mind freely, in talk and on paper.

Though somewhat older than Diodati, Milton went to Cambridge two years later than his friend went to Oxford; however, being some months past sixteen, he was within the average span of age, fifteen to eighteen. He was admitted to Christ's College on February 12, 1625, matriculated on April 9, and apparently began residence in that Easter term. During his time at Cambridge the number of students, tutors, and others was about three thousand, a higher figure than was ever reached again before 1900. Milton's college had some 260 persons, and in that small community he would doubtless become acquainted with all his fellow students. Two of these were John Cleveland, who was destined to win great fame or notoriety as a poet and satirist of extravagantly "metaphysical" wit, and Henry More, who entered in 1631 and was to be a leader of Cambridge Platonism. There is no evidence to show whether Milton knew such contemporaries in other colleges as Roger Williams (whom he did know later), Thomas Randolph, Thomas Fuller, Jeremy Taylor, Richard Crashaw, and George Herbert, who in July, 1626, made his last speech as Public Orator.

Although the academic curriculum had been somewhat leavened by Renaissance humanism, and could be by individual tutors, the main pattern and substance were still Aristotelian. The four-year undergraduate program commenced with logic and added ethics, physics, and metaphysics. Whether such study was narrow, repetitious, and barren or relatively broad and stimulating depended a good deal on both tutor and pupil. There was a mixture of private and public exercises. The day began with chapel at five, and that was followed by tutorial sessions, lectures, and disputations, which went through the early afternoon. There was leisure for the various diversions, high or low, of collegiate youth in all ages. In the autumn of 1626 Milton must have needed some, since—though his little epic *On the Fifth of November* may have been written in the long vacation—bishops and Cambridge officials were dying at a rate that taxed his Latin muse.

One episode of the spring of 1626 is not fully clear. Milton had been assigned to William Chappell, who was by far the most popular tutor at Christ's. John Aubrey, reporting information from Milton's brother Christopher, said: "His first tutor there was Mr. Chapell; from whom receiving some unkindness (whipped him), he was afterwards (though it seemed contrary to the rules of the college) transferred to the tuition of one Mr. Tovell. . . ." This story (in which the whipping seems improbable) was taken over by Dr. Johnson and has long been an item in Miltonic biography. Although it has been questioned and although data are meager, there seems no good reason to doubt that in the spring of 1626, at the end of his first year, Milton was sent down or rusticated for part of the Lent term. In addition to Aubrey, evidence that skeptics can hardly get around is in Milton's Elegy 1, addressed to Diodati. At home in London, he says that he is not eager to return to Cambridge, that he has no love for his forbidden abode, a place very uncongenial to votaries of poetry; he is not disposed to go on enduring the threats of a harsh tutor and other indignities his spirit cannot bear; meantime his exile—so much more pleasant than his beloved Ovid's—leaves him free for the diversions which he happily describes; but he is soon to go back to marshy Cambridge and the hoarse murmur of the classroom. The friction between Chappell and his

freshman pupil may have been temperamental or intellectual or both. At any rate the College authorities
appear not to have considered Milton notably at fault,
since, despite the rules, he was transferred to another
tutor and graduated in the usual time.

When he took his B.A. in 1629 Milton was one of 259;
of these only twenty-four were what we would call
Honors graduates, and Milton was fourth on the list, the
highest of the four men from Christ's. He continued three
years longer at Cambridge. Requirements for the M.A.
seem to have been rather vague, and perhaps should be
called opportunities, since candidates were much less
subject to curricular obligations. Milton may have spent
a good part of his time on Hebrew, Greek, Latin, Italian,
music, mathematics, history, and geography. When he
took his second degree in July, 1632, he was at the head
of the twenty-seven men from Christ's College. This and
other bits of evidence indicate that he was later well
warranted in saying, in reply to false accusations, that he
left Cambridge "not without affectionate regret on the
part of most Fellows of the College, who had shown me
many marks of their esteem" (*Second Defence*).

Latin Prose and Verse

B EFORE WE COME to the Latin and English poems of
the Cambridge years we must glance at Milton's
academic speeches or prolusions, which, if not always
on topics that he would have chosen, tell us something
of his intellectual interests and attitudes. Disputations—
a partial equivalent of modern examinations—were Latin
speeches for or against a given proposition. They started
on a small, informal scale in tutorial groups and, as students—or the abler ones—advanced, debates became
public affairs in the college or before a university audience. (Such disputations, by the way, were naturally
carried on at seventeenth-century Harvard.) The young
speaker was expected to show command of good Latin,
the rhetorical and logical arts of persuasion, general
learning, and skill in delivery. Such capacities might be
demonstrated even on such a theme as that of Milton's
first and mainly mythological prolusion, "Whether Day
is more excellent than Night," a theme more appropriate,
as he says, to verse than prose, and one not unrelated to
L'Allegro and *Il Penseroso*. Prolusion 2, "On the Music of
the Spheres," develops a familiar Pythagorean idea very
congenial to a Platonist and musician; in the *Nativity*,
Arcades, and *At a Solemn Music* it takes the very Miltonic
form of musical harmony as a symbol of concord between

earth and heaven. Prolusion 3 is a Renaissance humanist's
attack on the sterility of scholastic logic and a plea for
the humanities and science which was to be amplified
in Prolusion 7. The fourth and fifth pieces are grimly
resolute exercises on Aristotelian and scholastic topics,
relieved at moments by extraneous allusions; while the
speaker is not sure whether he is boring his hearers, he
is, he declares, certainly boring himself.

Prolusions 6 and 7 are of special interest. The sixth was
delivered at a holiday assembly in July, 1628. Though
pressed unexpectedly into service as "Father" or "Dictator" and taken away from his literary pursuits, Milton, in
the first half of his speech, was led by the festive occasion, his role, and the evidence of his growing popularity,
into personal and humanistic expansiveness. The second
half, on the assigned theme, is less attractive: Milton's
nature did not lend itself to the labored and sometimes
crude wit expected at a holiday gathering. At one point
he flares up to repudiate the nickname of "the Lady"
(*Domina*) which his fair complexion and moral strictness had drawn upon him. At the end come the English
verses printed as *At a Vacation Exercise*.

The seventh and last Prolusion, whatever its date
(1631–1632?), is at once a valedictory to Cambridge and
a vision of a brave new world, a tissue of humanistic
commonplaces enlarged and vitalized by impassioned
personal feeling and magnanimous ambition. The Christian Platonist sees man's immortal mind becoming godlike in its quest of universal knowledge and wisdom, a
goal attainable only by the good. Through contemplation
and action great men become oracles and reformers of
nations. At this time Milton may or may not have read
Bacon; in any case he is thoroughly Baconian in his
picture of man's winning control over nature. The de-
featist doctrine of nature's decay—already repudiated in
a Latin poem—Milton puts into the mouth of dying

Ignorance; besides, if the term of earthly fame is to be cut short by the final conflagration, there is still the greater glory of heaven (a theme to be grandly reaffirmed in *Lycidas*).

Of the verse written during 1626–1629 that Milton was to print, about two-thirds (if orthodox dating is followed) were in Latin, one-third in English. Thus it was in Latin that he learned the elements of his craft, and his best poems of these and later years place him in the front ranks of Neo-Latinists. From the fourteenth through the earlier seventeenth century (to go no farther back or forward), the European Renaissance produced a huge mass of Latin verse which has long sunk below even the normal scholarly horizon, but it was of high importance in its own long period. To mention only a few names of special luster, some of which remain illustrious for other reasons, there were the Italian Petrarch, Poliziano, Pontano, Mantuan, Sannazaro, Castiglione, Vida, and Alciati, the Dutch Joannes Secundus and Grotius (the latter became a renowned jurist), the Polish Casimir Sarbiewski, the Scottish George Buchanan, the English Sir Thomas More, John Owen, Milton, Crashaw, Cowley, and others. Neo-Latin verse nourished classical studies and cultural solidarity, revived the classical genres, and refined aesthetic and technical perception. If much of it was only elegant formalism, so was much derivative verse in the modern languages. At any rate, up through the nineteenth century, Latin verse-making had its place in the education of most writers and readers.

The college bards of Milton's time were much given to publishing anthologies of mainly Latin verse celebrating events in the royal family, the universities, and the nation at large. Milton's most ambitious effort in the public line, done at the age of seventeen, was the miniature epic, *In quintum Novembris* (1626), a contribution, strongly anti-Catholic of course, to one of the annual

thanksgivings for deliverance from the Gunpowder Plot;
the picture of Satan is a forceful if very crude anticipation of *Paradise Lost*. Two short poems have philosophical themes: *Naturam non pati senium* (*That Nature Does
Not Suffer Decay*) and *De Idea Platonica quemadmodum
Aristoteles intellexit* (*On the Platonic Idea, as Aristotle
Understood It*). Either may be the piece Milton spoke of
in a letter to his friend Gill (July 2, 1628) as something
he had hastily written for the use of a college Fellow in
a Commencement disputation. The former—the more
likely one—reminds us of George Hakewill's big *Apology
of the Power and Providence of God* (1627; enlarged
1630, 1635), a landmark in the long debate between
deteriorationists and progressives. Whether or not Milton
had looked into the progressive Hakewill, he was on the
same side: in mythological rather than scientific terms
he denied the common pessimistic doctrine that nature,
including man, was in a perpetual process of decay. The
other poem, which has some affinity with the second
Prolusion, is a bit of half-grotesque irony: assuming the
role of a flat-footed Aristotelian, Milton questions Platonic
idealism, though his purpose is to vindicate Plato.

Apart from his growing technical accomplishment, the
prime interest of Milton's Latin verse is the revelation
of personal feelings that he was willing to make in a
learned language, in the especially congenial elegiac
meter, and in epistles to such an intimate friend as
Diodati. In the *Apology for Smectymnuus* (1642) Milton
recalled his early love for "the smooth elegiac poets . . .
Whom both for the pleasing sound of their numerous
[i.e. metrical] writing, which in imitation I found most
easy and agreeable to nature's part in me, and for their
matter, which what it is, there be few who know not,
I was so allured to read that no recreation came to me
better welcome." The elegiac meter of alternating hexameters and pentameters was identified chiefly with the

amatory verse of Ovid (who used it also for his *Fasti*
and poems of exile), Propertius, and Tibullus, and such
moderns as Buchanan. Milton's seven Elegies were only
in part erotic, and never in the Roman sense. The obitu-
ary poem on Lancelot Andrewes (autumn, 1626) begins—
like the one on the bishop of Ely written just after it—as
a conventional exercise but unfolds a vision of heaven
which is a foretaste of *Lycidas*; the last line apparently
echoes Ovid's and Tibullus' prayerful visions of another
encounter with Corinna and Delia. In Elegy 4 (1627),
addressed to Thomas Young in Hamburg, now threatened
by approaching armies, Milton reveals incipient Puritanism in his sympathetic picture of his old tutor as a religious exile. In Elegy 1, the earliest (spring, 1626), as we
have seen, he links himself with another kind of exile,
the Ovid who wrote so many complaints from the shore
of the Black Sea; and the Cambridge Milton is banished
from is as unfavorable to poetry as the Crimea Ovid was
banished to. But, free for the time to please himself,
Milton rejoices in the "books that are my life," in plays,
and the sight of lovely girls. This last theme evokes a
youthfully extravagant and no doubt half-playful rhetoric
which does not hide his real intensity of feeling, an
intensity none the less real for the moral control symbolized by the divine plant that had saved Odysseus from
Circe.

Elegy 7 (May 1, 1627 or 1628) is a fuller revelation
of Milton's susceptibility to feminine beauty. Arrogantly
scornful of love, the young poet, at dawn on May Day,
is visited by the angry Cupid, who boasts of his power
over gods and heroes and promises revenge. Then the
poet, walking in the park and again meeting groups of
starry girls, is overcome by the loveliness of one of them;
he gazes, she passes on, and ecstasy turns into despair.
No encounter was ever more innocent; what matters is

not the magnitude of the stimulus but the quality of the response.

By far the best of Milton's early Latin poems is Elegy 5, *On the Coming of Spring* (1629). Stimulated by the season, his intoxicated senses riot in a panorama of re-awakening life and love in nature and man. Cupid is now more than the blind bow-boy; he has his larger role of cosmic force, as the true son of the Lucretian Venus. Even the mythological images that render the processes of nature are strongly sexual. Yet what at first sight may appear a formless effusion is firmly molded. Milton begins by invoking the nightingale as his companion in song and then describes in order the effects of spring in the heavens, on the sun-warmed earth, and on earth's children, the throngs of young men and women in love with love and one another. The earth lures even the amorous gods from heaven; and wanton Pan, Faunus, the satyrs, dryads, and oreads are all pursuing or pursued. The poem ends with a prayer that the divinities may long stay in their terrestrial haunts and bring back the golden age. It is a completely pagan poem, with no trace of moral or religious tension; the young poet is fully alive to the demands of "decorum." The allusive rhetoric does not here call attention to itself; rather, it is powerfully functional in its heady rendering of untamed natural impulse. At the same time the assured artistic control implies that moral control is there too, even if it is temporarily in abeyance.

In Elegy 6 (December–January, 1629–1630) the innocent neopagan gives way to the aspiring poet-priest. Charles Diodati, visiting in the country, had apologized for the quality of verses he had sent, on the ground that Christmastide festivities were unfavorable to the muses. In the first half of his reply Milton sympathetically develops the text that song loves Bacchus and Bacchus loves song, moving from the vinous inspiration of some classical poets down to Diodati and dances and the gay elegy. But then, as if shifting to the opposite side in a disputation, he celebrates heroic themes, whose votaries must lead blameless lives of ascetic simplicity, like Pythagoras and Greek poets and prophets. And he ends with a summary of an English poem he has just written, the *Nativity.**

From childhood Milton's scholarly tastes and talents had marked him out, in his elders' eyes and his own, for a clerical career, but in his own mind that idea must have weakened before he left Cambridge; when he reached a definite decision we do not know. The reason he later gave, hostility toward the prelatical church, was doubtless combined with a growing sense of his poetic vocation. The former motive does not appear, the latter is stressed, in the poem *Ad Patrem*. This piece has been dated by scholars over a wide span of years (the favored date being about 1637), but the natural time for discussing the choice of a profession would be Milton's last terms at Cambridge, 1631–1632, and the tone and details support that view. The addressing of his father in Latin was itself a quietly adroit reminder of the literary education he had been given and of the cultural bonds between them. A practitioner of the art of music cannot scorn the divine role of poetry or object to a son's devo-

---

* When Milton's poems were published, Elegy 7, though not, by his own dating, the latest of the elegies, was placed last in the group; it was followed by a ten-line apology for these monuments of his wantonness and an assurance that, thanks to Plato, his breast was now encased in ice that Cupid and Venus could not penetrate. Such an apology would have been quite inappropriate after Elegy 6, the latest of the series, whereas the erotic Elegy 7 links itself with Elegy 5 and the partly erotic Elegy 1; and the reference to Plato corresponds to the reference to the herb moly (temperance) at the end of Elegy 1. Thus Milton was apparently at once recognizing the traditional character of elegiac verse and dismissing a phase of his own evolution.

tion to what he has been fitted for; and he is not pushing his son into sordidly gainful occupations like the law. Milton combines filial gratitude with gentle but firm insistence that his way, a perhaps immortal way, lies through poetry.

❖❮❖❮❮❖❮ 3 ❫❖❫❖❫❖❫❖

Early English Poems

MILTON'S FATHER, as we saw, had contributed tunes to a psalmbook of 1621, and his own earliest extant verses in English are paraphrases of Psalms 114 and 136 done, according to his printed note, when he was fifteen. They were his first efforts in a kind of writing engendered by the Reformation and fostered by an impulse to provide better versions for congregational and family singing than the old ones of Sternhold and Hopkins (who, as Fuller said, had drunk more of Jordan than of Helicon). All sorts of writers tried their hand—Sir Philip Sidney (in whose versions has been seen a germ of "metaphysical" poetry), King James, Bacon, George Wither (whose *Hymns and Songs of the Church* of 1623 were given official standing by royal patent), George Sandys, and even the courtly and licentious Thomas Carew. The young Milton's vigorous versions show already his eager response to the wonders of God's power and providence, the faith that was to be his chief or only support through many dark years. They show too the influence of Josuah Sylvester's high-flown and very popular translation of Du Bartas' Protestant epic of creation, *Divine Weeks and Works* (completed in 1608); and some phrases may come from the Latin version of the Psalms by George Buchanan.

Milton's earliest original poem in English, *On the Death of a Fair Infant Dying of a Cough*, which commemorated his sister Anne's baby daughter—she died in January, 1628—is a much fuller index to his youthful taste. Of the three main poetical currents flowing in the 1620's, those identified with the names of Spenser, Donne, and Jonson (the latter two often ran together), it was the oldest, the mellifluous decorative vein, that attracted Milton. His voice here is a thin treble in comparison with the resonant *Nativity*, and his structural sense is uncertain, but, in carrying over mythological reference and rhetoric from his Latin obituaries, he attempted a more complex contrast between the inadequacy of the pagan view of death and the full assurance of Christian consolation.

A few months later, in the summer of 1628, Milton wrote the English verses, printed in 1673 as *At a Vacation Exercise*, which formed part of his sixth Prolusion. The genial and expansive disclosure of his own interests, which we noted in the first half of his speech, is continued in the poem. In heroic couplets of some colloquial roughness Milton—who had so far written almost wholly in Latin—hails his neglected native language. He puts aside "those new-fangled toys and trimming slight" of some mannered Cambridge poetasters to affirm his larger conception of poetry, and one line and a half would not be out of place in *Paradise Lost*:

> Such where the deep transported mind may soar
> Above the wheeling poles. . . .

His graver subjects include both the phenomena of nature and such heroic tales

> as the wise Demodocus once told
> In solemn songs at king Alcinous' feast.

Milton's imaginative and artistic capacity for an exalted theme was amply proved a year and a half later, just after his twenty-first birthday, by the composition of one of the great English odes, *On the Morning of Christ's Nativity*. Whatever his private, unrecorded ventures, the apprentice emerges suddenly as an assured master. In conception, ordered development, and ordered exuberance of rhythm, the poem had no English predecessor or successor. The stanzaic forms and the texture are the culmination of Milton's early Spenserian phase, but his originality is characteristic and complete; those for whom the word has a meaning may call the poem baroque.

In the prelude Milton launches the paradox of the Incarnation and, for the first time, asks if the Heavenly Muse will give him aid,

> Now while the heav'n, by the sun's team untrod,
>   Hath took no print of the approaching light,
> And all the spangled host keep watch in squadrons bright?
>
> See how from far upon the eastern road
> The star-led wizards haste with odors sweet!
> O run, prevent them with thy humble ode,
> And lay it lowly at his blessed feet. . . .

These few and singing lines are an example of the economical, effortless, "unmetaphysical" subtlety which, throughout Milton's work, can underlie apparent decorative simplicity. He is writing at home in 1629, before dawn on Christmas morning (the classical sun-god has not yet appeared), but time and space are annihilated: the stars still shining above dark London become the angelic host above Bethlehem, and the poet, or his Heavenly Muse, runs with a gift ahead of the three wise men on the eastern road. This telescoping of time continues to the end of the poem, as the mixed tenses indicate.

Milton's theme is not the human story of the Nativity but the significance of the Incarnation. The Hymn has three movements. The first seven stanzas show all nature,

earth and sea, stars and sun, awaiting, conscious of imperfection, the advent of the Creator. The conceits—even
if the first one, on the wintry earth denuded of foliage, is
a bit strained—do not come under the modern label of
"the pathetic fallacy"; that has no place in the old religious conception of animate nature as the art of God.
And, since Christ now enters history, Milton uses the
tradition that the whole Roman world was at peace. The
second movement begins with the gossiping shepherds
and the burst of angelic music. The music recalls the first
supreme event, the creation, "when of old the sons of
morning sung," and the birth of Christ foretells the third
event, the day of judgment which will inaugurate eternal
bliss. But that bliss begins now, with the incarnation of
grace on earth, and the first stage in the defeat of Satan
is the overthrow of the pagan gods. This exultant and
clangorous passage, the third movement, is the first
bravura display of Milton's manipulation of exotic names
and associations; the falseness of misguided worship, of
crude or cruel idolatry, can in no real sense be mitigated
by such beauty as, in stanza 20, takes us back to the
"paganism" of Elegy 5. In this poem we have too the first
of Milton's many perfect endings: the new bond between
heaven and earth is simply and obliquely affirmed in a
final—and pictorial—paradox:

> And all about the courtly stable
> Bright-harnessed angels sit in order serviceable.

No reader can miss the poem's unified structure and
jubilant rhythm, but it would take many pages to show
the allusive and symbolic density of the texture and the
working of the images of light and music (order) and
darkness and noise (disorder). The young poet's learning
and imagination stimulate and sustain each other, and his
religious faith, if as yet immature and untried, inspires
both. The poem has been called Milton's "Messianic

eclogue," and one of its ancestors is Virgil's fourth eclogue, which was throughout the Middle Ages taken as a prophecy of the birth of Christ: the Virgilian golden age is touched in Milton's stanza 14, and—a typical blending—Justice (Astraea) is to return along with the Mercy and Truth of Psalm 85. The poem as a whole is Milton's first English rendering of his lifelong vision of perfection.

The Passion, evidently associated with Holy Week of 1630, was broken off as a self-confessed failure. Milton was clearly not possessed by his theme as he had been in the *Nativity* and he wrote—sometimes beautifully—all around it. It may be that a sense of having overreached himself led him in this spring to the writing of a group of amatory poems, "O nightingale" and five sonnets and a canzone in Italian, though these poems have also been assigned to the earlier time of Elegies 7 and 5. "O nightingale," Milton's first English sonnet, is a quite artificial and quite charming presentation of zealous unsuccess in love; he makes gracefully humorous use of the medieval fancy that love will be auspicious if in the spring the nightingale's song is heard before the cuckoo's. The Italian poems show Milton's willingness to deal with amorous emotions and his considerable mastery of the language of idealistic love; they range from the conventionality of the fifth sonnet to the comparative originality of the canzone and the sixth sonnet. But chiefly the poems are a concrete reminder of the Italian influences which, directly or indirectly, were more or less important from the *Nativity* to *Samson*. It may be noted that in December, 1629, Milton bought a volume—now in the New York Public Library—containing Dante's *Convivio*, Giovanni della Casa's works, and Benedetto Varchi's sonnets; and he may have written the Italian poems about that time, if we accept the recent suggestion that the last two lines of Elegy 6 refer to verses done in Diodati's ancestral language.

Several very different pieces may be recorded before we look at a series that constitutes a distinct phase. Thomas Hobson, the aged carrier who for six decades had plied weekly between Cambridge and London (and whose practice in hiring out horses from his livery gave birth to the phrase "Hobson's choice"), died on January 1, 1631. Milton was one of many Cantabrigians who essayed more or less affectionately jocose elegies on the familiar veteran. His two colloquial contributions, strings of puns and gags, were included in comic anthologies in 1640 and 1658.

The many apparent echoes of Shakespeare in Milton's earlier poems are in some sense validated by both the reference in *L'Allegro* and the sixteen-line poem *On Shakespeare* which he dated 1630. This piece had the honor—how it came about is not known—of appearing in the Second Folio of 1632, so that it was the first English verse of Milton's to be printed. Like most short tributes of the kind, this has a lapidary generality, but it has also touches of personal feeling. Milton fixes on what was becoming a critical commonplace, Shakespeare's natural genius as contrasted with "slow-endeavoring art" which was so often—though not here—identified with Ben Jonson.

But the scholarly Milton likewise admired the scholarly Jonson, whose "learned sock" was linked in *L'Allegro* with Shakespeare's "native wood-notes wild," and in his next few poems his Spenserianism was overlaid by the rational, courtly urbanity of the Jonsonian lyrical style. The transition may be illustrated by the little *Song: On May Morning* (1629–1630?). This miniature ceremonial poem, written as if for choral singing, has a four-line prelude, a four-line hymn, and a two-line conclusion. The personifications of the prelude might be called Spenserian but are much more restrained than, say, the gorgeous painting of the dawn in *The Faerie Queene*, I.v.2; and the middle section—

> Hail, bounteous May, that dost inspire
> Mirth and youth and warm desire . . . —

is at once a subdued distillation of Elegy 5 and, in rhythm and style, an anticipation of *L'Allegro*.

The first elaborate example of Milton's semi-Jonsonian manner was the *Epitaph on the Marchioness of Winchester*. The Marchioness died on April 15, 1631, and Jonson himself wrote an elegy. It is not known if Milton, a student at Cambridge, had any connections with the family—a Catholic family, by the way. At any rate he feels the death of a young wife and mother who combined patrician rank with beauty of character, and he combines courtly and religious eulogy—not without the Miltonic image of heavenly light. Along with classical allusion there is some metaphysical wit (as in lines 31–34). We may be reminded of Henry King's magnificent *Exequy* by such a couplet as

> After so short time of breath
> To house with darkness and with death;

and another,

> Gentle Lady, may thy grave
> Peace and quiet ever have,

may echo the dirge in *Cymbeline*:

> Quiet consummation have,
> And renowned be thy grave!

L'Allegro and *Il Penseroso* were probably written in Milton's last long vacation from Cambridge, the summer of 1631. Like the *Epitaph*, they are in fluid couplets of seven or eight syllables and have a similar mixture of trochaic and iambic lines. The poems are the fine flower of Milton's discipleship to Jonson, but in quality of vision and in delicate grace and charm of phrase and rhythm and tone the poet of twenty-two excels his master. He is more Jonsonian, and perhaps more fully at ease, in the picture of social and mundane Mirth than in the less concrete and more exalted *Il Penseroso*—though the sixth Elegy's antithesis between the aesthetic and the ascetic is here relaxed. Of course the *persona* of both poems is a young man of highly cultivated sensibility who, like Milton, could enjoy both moods. But he maintains a "classical" impersonality. Classical, too, is the use of generalized particulars; the plowman is not a Wordsworthian Simon Lee whose weak ankles swell, but a symbolic figure in a landscape. And the classical artist reveals himself in the selective molding of all details into a unified whole.

From prelude to conclusion the twin poems are full of parallels and contrasts, though none of these are mechanical or forced. The abstract themes, Mirth and Melancholy (the latter is really Contemplation), are given general definition and a mythic genealogy, and then developed in terms of the occupations of an ideal day and night. The cheerful man is the observer of what goes on in country and city from dawn to late evening, the thoughtful solitary is seen—by us—from late afternoon to dawn; but these spans of time take in more than one season. Unity of tone within the individual poems and within the contrasted pair allows broad variety of reference. Rural sights and sounds range from

> many a youth and many a maid
> Dancing in the chequered shade

to the far-off curfew

> Over some wide-watered shore,
> Swinging slow with sullen roar.

Indoor scenes embrace cottage groups telling fairy tales, courtly tournaments and weddings, comedies on the London stage, and the lonely student reading Plato and Greek tragedy, Chaucer and romance; there is the music of gay lyrics and of cathedral anthems. Outer and inner worlds—"inner" including mental interiors—are alike civilized and idealized, though never sentimentalized. Various analogues have been noted, from Elizabethan praises of country life to the verses Robert Burton prefixed to the third edition (1628) of the *Anatomy of Melancholy*; and, whether or not Milton thought of it, the poems partake of a number of literary genres, the pastoral, the encomium, the emblem, the prose "character," the academic debate (the thoughtful student is clearly the author of the seventh Prolusion). But none of these things matter much in relation to the felicity of Milton's art and the purity of imagination, at once urbane and ethereal, that comprehends both social pleasures and religious ecstasy in a single vision. Mirth as well as Contemplation is an earthly reflection of heaven. Thinking of the later strenuous Milton, we may see both poems as a farewell to golden youth.

PART TWO

At Home
And Abroad

1632–1639

Minor Poems and *Comus*

IN MILTON'S SKETCH of his life in the *Second Defence of the English People* (1654) he says that on leaving Cambridge he returned home:

At my father's house in the country, where he had retired to pass his old age, I was free to give myself wholly to reading the Greek and Latin authors, though I sometimes paid a visit to London either to buy books or to learn something new in mathematics or music, in which at that time I found recreation. In this way I lived for five years.

His father's house was at Horton in Buckinghamshire, near Windsor, and these five and two-thirds years (1632–1638) are the so-called "Horton period." The traditional phrase remains usable for this part of Milton's career, although legal documents seem to indicate that in 1631–1632 the Miltons left the Cheapside house for semirural Hammersmith and lived there for a time before they moved to Horton.

Whatever the father's misgivings, to be read in and between the lines of *Ad Patrem*, he evidently acquiesced in his son's not seeking a professional means of livelihood. In his postbaccalaureate years at Cambridge Milton may have had more time to follow his own interests, but at home he could now settle down to mature and systematic study of the humanities, history, literature, and philosophy, presumably science, and, as he says, mathematics and music. His zeal, motives, and large vision may be inferred from the impassioned seventh Prolusion: the Renaissance humanist and poet-priest would master all learning and thought. It was in these years of ardent study that Milton's liberal thinking began to take shape and to gain solid intellectual and philosophical content.

Yet that he himself sometimes had misgivings, on a higher plane than his father's, is made very clear by the two poems which, so to speak, put the Horton period in a chronological frame, Sonnet 7 and *Lycidas*. When Milton wrote the sonnet—almost certainly not on his twenty-third but on his twenty-fourth birthday, December 9, 1632—he had been at home for half a year. However strong his belief in full preparation for his unknown future, he could hardly avoid feeling the difference between his recent past and the present. In the world of his college and the larger world of the university he had come to be a figure of recognized intellectual and literary distinction; now he is an obscure solitary at home, with nothing tangible to show for his months of study, while his academic contemporaries—or such juniors as his friend Diodati—are forging ahead. Also, he had perhaps written little poetry in more than a year, though the uncertainty of dates allows only guesses about that. With these things in mind, and the parable of the talents, Milton thus took stock of himself:

How soon hath Time, the subtle thief of youth,
 Stol'n on his wing my three and twentieth year!*

* That is, his first twenty-three years. In dating a number of his published Latin poems in the form of "Anno aetatis 17," Milton seems—according to an orthodox though sometimes disputed view—to have meant "At the age of seventeen," not "In his seventeenth year." Titles for this sonnet which include "the Age of Twenty-three" are late editorial additions and have no authority.

 In line 13, "All is, if" means "All depends on whether."

My hasting days fly on with full career,
But my late spring no bud or blossom shew'th.
Perhaps my semblance might deceive the truth,
That I to manhood am arrived so near,
And inward ripeness doth much less appear,
That some more timely-happy spirits endu'th.
Yet be it less or more, or soon or slow,
It shall be still in strictest measure ev'n
To that same lot, however mean or high,
Toward which Time leads me, and the will of Heav'n;
All is, if I have grace to use it so,
As ever in my great Task-Master's eye.

Milton, brought up from childhood in Christian faith and practice, could not experience "conversion" in the sense of a change of heart and behavior; but the word might also describe a mature and conscious dedication of one's self to God's service. While the *Nativity*, written just after Milton's coming of age, had been a kind of indirect self-consecration, the sonnet is direct and personal, and the plainness of the language and imagery is in keeping with the substance. It is typical of the author that the humble resolution and prayer of the sestet should, as it apparently does, echo Pindar's fourth Nemean ode: "But whatever excellence Lord Destiny gave me, I well know that the passage of time will bring it to its appointed perfection." Early in 1633 Milton wrote, and rewrote, a letter in English to a friend—possibly Thomas Young—who had counseled him against his seeming indulgence in mere study and withdrawal from active life and work, the ministry in particular. In it Milton copied the sonnet as proof that "I am something suspicious of myself, and do take notice of a certain belatedness in me." None the less, when he soberly weighs his motives in the letter, he is resolved to make himself fully fit for whatever work he is to do, however late he may enter the vineyard. The church may still be a possibility, although by this time it can hardly have been a very real one; between the lines both the sonnet and the letter suggest that he has already decided on another kind of service, the poetic priesthood to which his gifts and instincts lead him.

The chief first fruits of this state of mind appear to have been the two short poems, *On Time* and *At a Solemn Music* (1632-1633). To think of time—and the closely related theme of mutability and death—in Renaissance literature, or in English alone, is to make a mental anthology of great writing, from Spenser, Nashe, Shakespeare, Ralegh, Donne, Marvell, Browne, and others, a body of verse and prose that poignantly acknowledges the devouring of youth and beauty and love and may stress naturalistic acceptance or defiance of time or the religious consolation of eternity. Milton, as we might expect, is wholly absorbed in the Christian and Platonic vision. Both poems develop—in a different sequence—the contrast between the flux and dross of earth and the stability and perfection of heaven; the second poem is of course built on the musical metaphor of discord and harmony. In form each poem, a paragraph with lines of irregular length, is a madrigal or what might be one stanza of a canzone. In style they are neither Spenserian nor Jonsonian but impressively Miltonic, though their slowness of pace is unique; the manipulation of the irregular lines and rhythms gives weight to almost every syllable and a full fresh depth of meaning to even commonplace words.

The same contrast, and the same crystal purity of vision and tone, appear in the more fluid opening lines of *Comus*, of a year and a half later. But we must turn back to Milton's initial experiment with the masque, the graceful miniature *Arcades*. This is the first and presumably the earliest item in the invaluable Cambridge or Trinity College manuscript in which Milton kept copies of minor poems later than his juvenilia; it is followed there by the *Solemn Music* (three drafts), the letter to a friend mentioned above, *On Time*, and the rest. *Arcades* is commonly dated within 1630–1633 and some opinion favors 1632.* It was presented in honor of the Dowager Countess of Derby (she was known by the title of her first husband), who had long before received a dedication from her distant relative, Spenser, and who in 1600 had married Sir Thomas Egerton (the employer at that time of John Donne). The Countess's home, Harefield, was about ten miles from Horton (in 1630–1633, as we saw, the Miltons may not have been living there). *Arcades* was almost certainly produced, and Milton engaged to write it, by Henry Lawes, who, as a London musician of growing prominence, may well have known the Miltons. In 1630 he was appointed a "Gentleman of the Chapel Royal and Member of the King's Private Music"; he was also tutor in music to the family of the Countess's stepson, Sir John Egerton (who in 1617 became Earl of Bridgewater and in 1634 was the *raison d'être* of *Comus*).

Masques were a favorite and costly form of entertainment at the courts of James and Charles and at noble houses. They were composed largely of spectacle, music, and dancing, strung on some sort of allegorical and often mythological "device"; of drama, in the usual sense, there was little or nothing. *Arcades* falls about as far short of the average in length as *Comus* goes beyond it. After an introductory lyric a monologue is spoken by the Genius of the Wood, and two concluding lyrics lead the performers to the throne of the "rural queen," the Countess, and urge "Nymphs and Shepherds" of the mythic Arcadia

* We may exclude some time before and after May 14, 1631, when the Countess of Derby's son-in-law, the second Earl of Castlehaven, was executed "for unnatural offences" (Howell, *State Trials*, III, 401–426).

to move from Greece to England and live under her sway. Milton would naturally have in mind the great master of the masque, Ben Jonson, and his songs, songs of highly sophisticated modulations, have some audible echoes. The most characteristically Miltonic element in *Arcades* is the Platonic passage in the Genius's speech, on the music of the spheres as the heavenly harmony that keeps due order in the low world of unsteady nature.

In 1634, when Milton was twenty-five, his course of reading was pleasantly interrupted by another commission which again took him into the aristocratic world and into partnership with Lawes. Another and greater event in the same noble family was the inauguration of the Earl of Bridgewater as Lord President of Wales, and *Comus*—in a version somewhat shorter than our text— was presented on September 29, 1634, as part of the festivities at Ludlow Castle in Shropshire. Lawes, the producer and composer of the music, was the Attendant Spirit. The roles of the two Brothers and the Lady were taken by the Earl's children, Viscount Brackley and Thomas and Lady Alice Egerton, aged eleven, nine, and fifteen respectively; the three had already had experience in masques at court. The *Mask*—the title *Comus* began to be used only when it was acted in the eighteenth century—was published in 1637 by Lawes, who said that he had been besieged for copies and also that the author was withholding his name. Milton must of course have agreed to publication. He must also have chosen the motto (from Virgil's second eclogue), which expressed a perfectionist's reluctance to appear in public before he felt ripe—*Eheu quid volui misero mihi! floribus Austrum Perditus* ("Alas, what wretchedness I have wished upon myself! In my madness I have let in the south wind upon my flowers").

We need not concern ourselves with the various "sources"—in addition to Homer and Ovid and Spenser—

that Milton may have drawn upon for his plot and courtly pastoralism, such as George Peele's *Old Wives' Tale*, John Fletcher's *Faithful Shepherdess*, and Erycius Puteanus' *Comus* (1608), a moral fable in Latin prose. There are naturally some slight family resemblances between Milton's *Comus* and other masques; and incidental echoes of Shakespeare are often heard. In taking as his villain a son of Circe and Bacchus who inherited his mother's powers, Milton was freshening the Renaissance preoccupation with her and her many sisters and cousins. No parable was more popular than the Homeric tale which had long been allegorized as an encounter between heroic virtue and sensual temptation: Tasso and Spenser (*The Faerie Queene*, II.xii) and even the light-hearted Ariosto had worked elaborate variations on it, and it was in Milton's mind from the end of his first Latin Elegy to *Samson Agonistes* (lines 934–935). George Sandys, in the allegorical commentary that he printed in 1632 along with his translation of Ovid's *Metamorphoses*, expounded the standard interpretation at length, and, whether or not Milton had looked into his work, a few of Sandys's comments are of interest:

Yet Ulysses could not lose his shape with the rest, who, being fortified by an immortal power, was not subject to mutation. For the divine and celestial soul, subsisting through the bounty of the Creator, can by no assault of nature be violated, nor can that be converted into a beast which so highly participates of reason. . . .

Circe's sensual charms, he proceeds, "are not to be resisted but by the divine assistance, Moly, the gift of Mercury, which signifies temperance. . . ." Men of "headstrong appetites, which revolt from the sovereignty of reason (by which we are only like unto God, and armed against depraved affection)," can never return into their country (from whence the soul deriveth her celestial original) unless disenchanted and cleansed from their former impurity. For as Circe's rod, waved over their heads from the right side to the left, presents those false and sinister persuasions of pleasure, which so much deforms them, so the reversion thereof, by discipline, and a view of their own deformity, restores them to their former beauties.

The Platonic tinge of Sandys leads us to what is by far the best introduction to *Comus* in particular and the early Milton in general, his own account, in the *Apology for Smectymnuus* (1642), of the growth of his ideal of chastity and the reading that nourished it. (He was, we may remember, defending himself against charges of immorality.) The initial statement of his youthful love for "the smooth elegiac poets," Ovid and others, was quoted above in the first chapter, and the rest of the passage must be given at length, with some omissions:

. . . if I found those authors anywhere speaking unworthy things of themselves, or unchaste of those names which before they had extolled, this effect it wrought with me: from that time forward their art I still applauded, but the men I deplored, and above them all preferred the two famous renowners of Beatrice and Laura, who never write but honor of them to whom they devote their verse, displaying sublime and pure thoughts, without transgression. And long it was not after when I was confirmed in this opinion, that he who would not be frustrate of his hope to write well hereafter in laudable things, ought himself to be a true poem, that is, a composition and pattern of the best and honorablest things; not presuming to sing high praises of heroic men or famous cities unless he have in himself the experience and the practice of all that which is praiseworthy. These reasonings, together with a certain niceness of nature, an honest haughtiness, and self-esteem either of what I was or what I might be (which let envy call pride), and lastly that modesty whereof, though not in the title page, yet here I may be excused to make some beseeming profession—all these, uniting the supply of their natural aid together, kept me still above those low descents of mind beneath which he must deject and plunge himself that can agree to saleable and unlawful prostitutions.

Next (for hear me out now, readers) that I may tell ye whither my younger feet wandered, I betook me among those lofty fables and romances which recount in solemn cantos the deeds of knighthood founded by our victorious kings, and from hence had in renown over all Christendom. There I read it in the oath of every knight, that he should defend to the expense of his best blood, or of his life if it so befell him, the honor and chastity of virgin or matron; from whence even then I learnt what a noble virtue chastity sure must be, to the defense of which so many worthies, by such a dear adventure of themselves, had sworn. . . . So that even those books which to many others have been the fuel of wantonness and loose living, I cannot think how, unless by divine indulgence, proved to me so many incitements, as you have heard, to the love and steadfast observation of that virtue which abhors the society of bordellos.

Thus, from the laureate fraternity of poets, riper years and the ceaseless round of study and reading led me to the shady spaces of philosophy, but chiefly to the divine volumes of Plato and his equal [i.e., contemporary], Xenophon: where, if I should tell ye what I learnt of chastity and love, I mean that which is truly so, whose charming cup is only virtue, which she bears in her hand to those who are worthy (the rest are cheated with a thick intoxicating potion which a certain sorceress, the abuser of love's name, carries about), and how the first and chiefest office of love begins and ends in the soul, producing those happy twins of her divine generation, knowledge and virtue. . . .

Last of all, not in time, but as perfection is last, that care was ever had of me, with my earliest capacity, not to be negligently trained in the precepts of Christian religion. This that I have hitherto related hath been to show that, though Christianity had been but slightly taught me, yet a certain reservedness of natural disposition, and moral discipline learnt out of the noblest philosophy, was enough to keep me in disdain of far less incontinences than this of the bordello. But having had the doctrine of Holy Scripture, unfolding those chaste and high mysteries, with timeliest care infused, that "the body is for the Lord, and the Lord for the body," thus also I argued to myself: that if unchastity in a woman, whom St. Paul terms the glory of man, be such a scandal and dishonor, then certainly in a man, who is both the image and glory of God, it must, though commonly not so thought, be much more deflowering and dishonorable; in that he sins both against his own body, which is the perfecter sex, and his own glory, which is in the woman, and, that which is worst, against the image and glory of God, which is in himself. Nor did I slumber over that place* expressing such high rewards of ever accompanying the Lamb with those celestial songs to others inapprehensible, but not to those who were not defiled with women, which doubtless means fornication; for marriage must not be called a defilement.

Thus Dante and Petrarch, the romances of knighthood (no doubt Tasso and Spenser in particular), and especially Plato (the name includes the tradition) and the Bible were prime factors in molding the Christian-Platonic idealism of *Comus*. That idealism was a world away from the usually spurious "Platonics" fashionable at court. The last of the quoted paragraphs makes explicit the Christian humanist's distinction between and fusion of the "moral discipline learnt out of the noblest philosophy" and Christian teaching, and the distinction and the fusion run through the masque. The Attendant Spirit is a Neoplatonic daemon whose function approaches that of a guardian angel. The Elder Brother—who uses the Platonic image of the soul's wings (375–380) and paraphrases from the *Phaedo* a passage on its corruption (463–475)—emphasizes "moral discipline," although of course, like Milton, he recognizes religious sanctions.

* The "place" is Rev. 14:1 f.

The Second Brother's reason and faith are alike immature. The Lady embodies both in their mature and
active cooperation. When in the central debate Comus
urges his specious arguments for the free use of Nature's
bounties, her counterargument for temperance and order
is mainly rational, though the dictate of "spare Temperance" is "holy" and in the Christian tradition. But Comus
had gone on with a *non sequitur*, the common plea of
Renaissance naturalism for sexual license, and in replying
to that, in the second half of her speech (779–799),* the
Lady rises with "sacred vehemence" to a religious defense
of "the sun-clad power of chastity." The potent epithet—
one of the many images of light—is a reminder that
chastity is not mere abstinence from vice but the Miltonic
vision of perfection, the Platonic and Christian love of
the good.

The final note is religious. The plant that is more medi-
cinal than the Homeric moly and has its part in the defeat
of Comus is presumably Christianized temperance (along
with the whole context there is perhaps a particular
transcendental overtone: "in another country" it bore a
bright golden flower, "but not in this soil"). The brothers,
however, fail to capture Comus and release the Lady
from his spells, and Sabrina, the virginal nymph of the
Severn River, must be invoked. Milton's decorative use of
the chief local legend seems both to round off a moral
victory already won and to symbolize the necessity of
grace as well as rational virtue. The epilogue, which in
some lines recalls the songs of Prospero's Ariel, is richly
symbolic, and in a modern manner: the partly clear,
partly uncertain meaning is given through allusions, with
almost no "prose statement." The beauties of nature,
which Comus had tainted, can now be joyously accepted.

* Lines 737–755 and 779–806 (and also 997 and 999–1011)
were not in the acting version and first appeared in the 1637
edition.

The cycle of physical generation is embodied in the love of Venus and Adonis as Spenser (*Faerie Queene*, III.vi) and other Platonists had treated it. And the marriage of Cupid and Psyche is Christian-Platonic love. Their children are not here the "knowledge and virtue" of the *Apology for Smectymnuus*—that power the masque has shown—but "Youth and Joy," which Comus had claimed for himself and his crew. And, since Comus had posed also as the champion of freedom, the conclusion reaffirms the true freedom that leads its votaries

> Higher than the sphery chime;
> Or if Virtue feeble were,
> Heav'n itself would stoop to her.

The last couplet crystallizes Milton's intense moral and religious idealism in a poetic incantation.

In this work, by far the longest he had yet written, Milton was, consciously or not, experimenting with style. We come on bits of delicate pastoralism or romantic imagining—

> And airy tongues that syllable men's names
> On sands and shores and desert wildernesses—

that recall *A Midsummer Night's Dream* and *The Tempest;* colloquial speech and rhythm and flamboyant rhetoric; half-metaphysical wit; moral statement in the vein of Augustan classicism; rhymed couplets in the midst of the predominant blank verse; even a section (277 f.) which catches exactly the manner of Greek stichomythy. Comus's opening lyric resembles *L'Allegro* in manner, but his false claims and inverted values ("We that are of purer fire"; "Us thy vowed priests") are a first sketch for the ironic treatment of Satan. Comus's central speech to the Lady on the lavish prodigality of Nature (706 f.), with its picture of the spawn of the sea, millions of spinning worms, the air darkened by the wings of birds, is a unique early example of crowded tactile and visual images, of the rendering of active immediacy of process, in contrast with Milton's normal presentation of a distilled, generalized result. He could not have produced such a texture if—as Elegy 5 and later accounts of Eden and creation amply prove—his imagination were not always excited by the theme of fecundity; yet the method has a distinct purpose here, not so much to describe potential surfeit in nature but to reveal the speaker's moral disorder.

One last comment may be made on a work that invites many. Nothing shows more clearly the severity of Milton's artistic conscience than his canceling of fourteen lines which originally followed the fourth line. The manuscript version of the Attendant Spirit's opening speech reads thus, in part:

> Before the starry threshold of Jove's court
> My mansion is, where those immortal shapes
> Of bright aërial spirits live insphered
> In regions mild of calm and serene air,
> Amidst th' Hesperian gardens, on whose banks,
> Bedewed with nectar and celestial songs,
> Eternal roses grow, and hyacinth,
> And fruits of golden rind, on whose fair tree
> The scaly-harnessed dragon ever keeps
> His unenchanted eye. . . .

The lovely lines after the fourth, with others, Milton cut out (he salvaged some images later in the masque) because, we may guess, the rich coloring of the traditional earthly paradise blurred the direct contrast he wished to make between the white purity of heaven and "the rank vapors of this sin-worn mold." That contrast, as we observed, was the theme of *On Time* and *At a Solemn Music*, and the whole masque is a semidramatic expansion of it, a hymn in praise of the beauty of good.

Comus does not appeal to those who believe that the devil has all the tunes.

The evolution of Milton's early manner could be partly outlined in his images of the sun. One bit in the *Nativity* that has been seen as a possible lapse is this:

> So when the sun in bed,
> Curtained with cloudy red,
>   Pillows his chin upon an orient wave. . . .

The fanciful conceit gives place in *L'Allegro* to a classical and rational image which may owe something of its high color to Shakespeare's "eastern gate, all fiery red" (*Midsummer Night's Dream*, III.ii.391):

> Right against the eastern gate,
> Where the great sun begins his state,
> Robed in flames and amber light,
> The clouds in thousand liveries dight. . . .

In Comus's opening speech the sun is setting, color subsides into twilight, and the classical image of Phoebus is blended (as it had been in Spenser's *Epithalamion*) with that of the sun in the nineteenth Psalm:

> And the gilded car of day
> His glowing axle doth allay
> In the steep Atlantic stream;
> And the slope sun his upward beam
> Shoots against the dusky pole,
> Pacing toward the other goal
> Of his chamber in the east.

Here the sun is giving place to the shades that invite the orgies of the bestial crowd; and throughout the masque light and darkness have their symbolic value. But all these early images of the sun are transcended in the climactic sinking and rising of "the day-star" in *Lycidas*.

2

Lycidas

THE THREE YEARS between *Comus* and *Lycidas* are largely a blank in the record. Milton was pursuing his private studies under his father's roof, but he apparently wrote almost nothing and other items are sparse. In a letter to Alexander Gill of December 4, 1634, he reports that he was suddenly moved to a bit of Greek verse, the first he had done since leaving school; this was the paraphrase of Psalm 114 which he printed in his *Poems* (an English paraphrase of this Psalm was the earliest piece included in the book). Milton also assures Gill that he will meet him in London "among the book-sellers." We remember his later reference, already quoted, to such excursions. If we can shake off our habit of seeing writers only in pictures of their gaunt old age, we can, with the aid of the portrait of 1629–1630* and

---

* While it has been believed that only copies exist of this, the so-called Onslow portrait, a painting acquired in 1961 by the National Portrait Gallery, appeared, after cleaning, to be perhaps the original (F. Davis, *Illustrated London News*, January 6, 1962). I have seen no further report. Cf. F. Davis, *ibid.*, July 22, 1961; George C. Williamson, *Milton Tercentenary. The Portraits, Prints and Writings of John Milton* (1908); J. M. French, *Life Records of John Milton* (bibliography below); John R. Martin, *The Portrait of John Milton at Princeton and its place in Milton Iconography* (Princeton University Library, 1961).

early biographers, imagine a trim, middle-sized, handsome young man, wearing a sword he knew how to use, browsing among the stalls in St. Paul's Churchyard.

A document that begins to be of service for these years is Milton's Commonplace Book (discovered in 1874), although a large proportion of the entries, including most of those on marriage and divorce, belong to 1640–1644; a few were made in 1645–1649, and more thereafter. Until he lost his sight in the winter of 1651–1652, Milton made these notes in his own hand. The keeping of such a book of extracts, with or without comments by the compiler, was a habit of the age; one famous example is Ben Jonson's *Timber*. Milton's notes do not begin to cover the full extent of his reading, but they take in some ninety authors and a hundred and ten works, and, so far as they go, they are a valuable guide to both his reading and his thinking. The notes are divided under three heads, moral, domestic, and political; a similar but separate collection on religion seems to have been lost. In the book as a whole, historians, ancient and modern, foreign and English, are greatly predominant, and yield moral and domestic as well as political entries. Church fathers are not inconspicuous. In the early years from about 1635 to about 1642, notes from miscellaneous writers include half a dozen from Dante and several from Sir Philip Sidney's *Arcadia*. One would never guess that the compiler was himself a poet; he seems rather to be a historian who, while ranging very widely, does not shrink from the most minute examples of political and ethical ideas. The book is a concrete, not to say gritty, testimony to the truth of Edward Phillips's phrase about Milton's "still prosecuting his studies and curious search into knowledge, the grand affair perpetually of his life."

In a Latin letter to Diodati of 1637—the date, September 23, in the printed text of 1674 probably should have been November 23—Milton wrote:

By continued reading I have brought the affairs of the Greeks to the time when they ceased to be Greeks. I have been occupied for a long time by the obscure history of the Italians under the Longobards, Franks, and Germans, to the time when liberty was granted them by Rudolph, King of Germany. From there it will be better to read separately about what each State did by its own effort.

This may sound as if the poet were in a fair way to stifle himself. Yet we must remember the Renaissance humanist's conception of the heroic poet as a universal scholar, already illustrated from Milton's youthful utterances and confirmed by his later insistence that to the religious purpose of poetry "must be added industrious and select reading, steady observation, insight into all seemly and generous arts and affairs." And there is ample reassurance, if it is needed, in earlier passages of the letter quoted just above:

For though I do not know what else God may have decreed for me, this certainly is true: He has instilled into me, if into anyone, a vehement love of the beautiful. Not so diligently is Ceres, according to the Fables, said to have sought her daughter Proserpina, as I seek for this idea of the beautiful, as if for some glorious image, throughout all the shapes and forms of things ("for many are the shapes of things divine"); day and night I search and follow its lead eagerly as if by certain clear traces. Whence it happens that if I find anywhere one who, despising the warped judgment of the public, dares to feel and speak and be that which the greatest wisdom throughout all ages has taught to be best, I shall cling to him immediately from a kind of necessity. . . . You ask what I am thinking of? So help me God, an immortality of fame. What am I doing? Growing my wings and practising flight. But my Pegasus still raises himself on very tender wings. Let me be wise on my humble level.*

* *Complete Prose Works,* ed. D. M. Wolfe *et al.,* I (Yale University Press, 1953), 326–327. The phrase in quotation marks appears at the end of several plays of Euripides.

This letter, recording Milton's study of obscure medieval history, his dream of immortal fame, and his present unripeness and diffidence, was written in the very month, or certainly within two months, of the composition of *Lycidas,* perhaps the greatest short poem in the language.

The immediate occasion was, as everyone knows, the drowning of Edward King in a shipwreck in the Irish Sea in August, 1637. He was the son of Sir John King, an English official in Ireland. He had entered Christ's College in 1626, at the age of fourteen, had taken his B.A. in 1630, had been designated by royal mandate for a fellowship, had received his M.A. in 1633, and had proceeded toward holy orders. He contributed some short and undistinguished Latin poems to Cambridge anthologies. Probably his early death and the nature of it helped to elicit from his associates a volume of elegies, a kind of honor commonly reserved for more important persons. *Justa Edouardo King* (1638) contained pieces in Latin, Greek, and English, three of them from Joseph Beaumont, John Cleveland, and Henry More; in general, and as usual, the elegies ranged from swollen rhetoric to flat or concave prose. *Lycidas* came at the end, signed "J. M." In the Cambridge Manuscript the poem was dated "Novemb: 1637," so that it was written just before Milton's twenty-ninth birthday.

Milton would have known King quite well, as he would have known many others in the small community of the college, but we have no reason to think there was any close connection; Edward Phillips's statement in 1694 of "a particular friendship and intimacy" sounds like a mere inference from the fact of Milton's having written an elegy. Anyhow, the actual degree of intimacy and hence of personal sorrow is quite irrelevant. Milton's mother had died in April, 1637, but the death of a junior contemporary came home to him in a very different way. King was a college associate, in some sense a poet, a virtuous young man destined for the priesthood which Milton had rejected, and his promising life was suddenly cut off before it had well begun. Milton had spent over five years in solitary study and obscurity, laboring to fit himself for service under his great Task-Master's eye and nursing a magnanimous ambition for immortal fame. He could hardly escape the paralyzing thought, "There, but for the grace of God, go I," and in such a thought "the grace of God" would not be an empty formula. We cannot understand the impact of King's death and Milton's impassioned response unless we realize his Christian premise, that no sparrow falls to the ground without God's will; this drowning was not a grievous accident, it was a positive act of God. Milton is wrestling with Job's question: why should the just man suffer? What is the nature of God's world in which such things happen? This inexplicable event, the first of its kind that has touched him, has cast a dark cloud over Milton's hitherto untested idealism and religious faith.

In spite of, or because of, his surging, struggling emotions, Milton was never a more completely classical artist than he is here, both in the particular sense of his using a genre of notably specific conventions and in the broad sense of generalized impersonality and detachment. *Lycidas* is at once an agonized personal cry and a formal exercise, a search for order and a made object, an affirmation of faith in Providence and an exploitation of pastoral and archetypal myth. With every reading the poem reveals more depths and complexities.

Modern readers may, like Dr. Johnson, sniff or snort at the pastoral convention, but it had enough vitality to last two thousand years; from the start Theocritus and Virgil had made it a dramatic vehicle for almost anything a poet wished to say. The ancient models for the special branch, the elegy, were Virgil's fifth eclogue (with which the tenth, though not an elegy, went along) and three less generally familiar Greek poems, Theocritus' first Idyll, Bion's *Epitaph for Adonis*, and the *Epitaph for Bion* attributed to Moschus; among the many Renaissance exemplars were Castiglione's *Alcon* and Spenser's *November* eclogue and *Daphnaida* and *Astrophel*. But *Lycidas* far surpasses all other pastoral elegies because Milton's feelings are deeply involved in a grand theme, and in seeking ordered expression his masterful artistry re-creates the conventions. Those conventions supply the means of development and control; the formal pattern, derived from the canzone, with its paragraphs and lines of irregular length and its interweaving of rhymes, provides for disciplined and subtle flexibility and freedom of maneuver.

Something of the character of the poem may be suggested by an outline, however bald. In the first paragraph the avowed unripeness of the poet and the fact of young Lycidas' death merge in the idea of unfulfillment. The association or identification becomes overt in the appeal to the Muses, in the allusion to "my destined urn" and "my sable shroud," and it is carried on, in a contrasted mood, in the picture of the two shepherds' pastoral life: this is carefree youth as it was before death struck one of the pair, and, too, this is nature in its normal order and serenity. Then the conventional mourning of nature for its dead singer turns into something else, the admission that nature has another side, that life contains the seeds of death, early death—the canker in the rose, the taintworm that destroys the weanling herds, the frost that kills spring flowers. This undertone of doubt and fear gathers momentum through vain questioning of the nymphs and explodes in the strident lines on the death of Orpheus, the archetypal poet, whom even his mother the Muse could not save.

The next paragraph, bringing the problem into the open, sways back and forth in a passionate dialectic. Why devote one's self to the arduous discipline of poetry instead of sensual pleasure? The answer is the hope of fame, "That last infirmity of noble mind." But the answer to that is that death—not God's providence but "the blind Fury with th' abhorred shears"—may end life before fame is won. To that the answer is a new definition of fame, not earthly glory but the true and lasting fame in heaven that is given by God's judgment on the quality of life, not its outward achievements. This assertion of Christian faith is to be the ultimate answer of the poem, yet it does not, at this stage, carry full conviction to either poet or reader, and it will not until the problem is further explored.

From this direct and central paragraph Milton returns to the pastoral mode. The procession of mourners, like other conventions, is transformed. The reports of the gods of the sea and the winds—that on the day of the wreck both water and air were calm—lead to execration of "that fatal and perfidious bark"; in other words, the poet gropes, in vain, for some natural cause (or expression through nature of the divine will). Camus, the representative of Cambridge, may seem purely conventional, yet his "Ah, who hath reft . . . my dearest pledge?" is part of the cumulative questioning of God's providence. The speech of the last mourner, St. Peter, is, like the passage on fame, a nominal digression, but this harsh and vehement invective—all in pastoral terms—brings out another aspect of God's unaccountable ways: while He cuts off the life of a worthy young cleric, He allows the grossly unworthy to infest His church. Milton may have had in mind such passages from Dante (*Inferno* xix, *Paradiso* xx), Petrarch (Sonnet cviii), Spenser (*May* eclogue), and others as he was to quote in his first and third tracts against the bishops. In this speech he first raised his Puritan standard: his attack on the clergy may have been stimulated by the brutal and notorious punish-

ment, in the summer of 1637, of the Puritan pamphlet-
eers, William Prynne, Henry Burton, and John Bastwick;
"the grim wolf" is presumably the Church of Rome and
may refer to recent conversions, especially in the circle
of Charles's French queen, Henrietta; and the last two
lines, whatever the precise meaning of the much-
discussed metaphor, are certainly a prophecy of God's
final judgment.

Upon this outburst follows the catalogue of flowers.
But the glowing picture of these half-animate mourners
carries a double irony: behind nature's beauty is still the
fact of nature's violence, and the summoning of the
flowers is vain because there is no laureate hearse to
strew them on. And that double consciousness erupts in
a volume of sound and allusion which brings home the
helplessness of puny man amid the elements that God
seems to leave uncontrolled:

> Ay me! whilst thee the shores and sounding seas
> Wash far away, where'er thy bones are hurled,
> Whether beyond the stormy Hebrides,
> Where thou perhaps under the whelming tide
> Visit'st the bottom of the monstrous world;
> Or whether thou, to our moist vows denied,
> Sleep'st by the fable of Bellerus old,
> Where the great Vision of the guarded mount
> Looks toward Namancos and Bayona's hold:
> Look homeward, Angel, now, and melt with ruth;
> And, O ye dolphins, waft the hapless youth.

But this final despair concerning the mortal body and
all earthly judgments gives place to the final triumph:

> Weep no more, woeful shepherds, weep no more,
> For Lycidas, your sorrow, is not dead,
> Sunk though he be beneath the wat'ry floor;
> So sinks the day-star in the ocean bed,
> And yet anon repairs his drooping head, .
> And tricks his beams, and with new-spangled ore

Flames in the forehead of the morning sky:
So Lycidas sunk low, but mounted high,
Through the dear might of him that walked the waves,
Where, other groves and other streams along,
With nectar pure his oozy locks he laves,
And hears the unexpressive nuptial song
In the blest kingdoms meek of joy and love.
There entertain him all the saints above,
In solemn troops and sweet societies
That sing, and singing in their glory move,
And wipe the tears for ever from his eyes. . . .

Complete reassurance has come, not with argument, but with a beatific vision, a full realization of death as rebirth. This was of course in the tradition of Christian elegy, but no poet before Milton had achieved anything like his imaginative, verbal, and rhythmical crescendo. The ordered process of nature can again be appealed to, in the analogy of the sun, and images of water, no longer woeful, reach a climax in the simple and tender periphrasis, "Through the dear might of him that walked the waves," an oblique reminder of the power and love that envelop human life and justify God's ways to men. With the vindication of life and death, and the reconciliation of nature and man, the poet subsides into a mood of pastoral acceptance. Lycidas, though a spirit in heaven, can be seen as a classical divinity of sea and shore who is a symbol and agent of divine mercy. The last paragraph is not merely a convention of the canzone, the poet's address to his own poem (exemplified in Spenser's *Epithalamion*): in setting off the elegy as a completed thing it completes the elegist's reconciliation with the actual world. Nature reassumes the benign regularity it had had before the tragic event, and the poet can leave mourning and questioning to face life with strength and hope. Like Milton's later quiet endings, this testifies to order attained through struggle.

3

Italian Travels

AFTER HIS MOTHER'S DEATH and nearly six years of studious reading, Milton gratified a desire to travel. Probably in May, 1638, he set off for Italy, with a servant, and armed with a letter of advice from old Sir Henry Wotton, once the ambassador to Venice and now Provost of Eton. In Paris the English ambassador furnished helpful letters of introduction. There Milton was enabled to meet the great humanist and jurist, Hugo Grotius, whose early Latin verse he had probably read. But Milton chose to spend most of his time in Italy, the traditional goal of the Renaissance humanist and the country to whose language and literature he was especially attached, although, as he said in *Areopagitica*, its cultural vitality had ebbed. He made two prolonged sojourns in both Florence and Rome. His interest seems to have been in persons and places—witness Vallombrosa—and literature rather than in the fine arts, but he was of course an eager observer of classical antiquities. St. Peter's may have given suggestions for the "neoclassical" palace of Pandemonium built by the devils in hell, and impressions of some paintings may also be imbedded in *Paradise Lost*. Through the friendly German scholar and Vatican librarian, Lukas Holste, Milton was invited to a spectacular pastoral opera given on February 27, 1639, by Cardinal Barberini at his palace. The libretto was by Rospigliosi, the stage design by Bernini. It was perhaps Milton's first hearing of an Italian *dramma per musica*. Among the boxes of books he sent home, one or two contained music, including some of Monteverdi, the chief of modern Italian composers and of pioneers in opera.

After the operatic hospitality the young Puritan made a courtesy call on the Cardinal and was graciously received. In spite of his anti-Catholicism, Milton associated freely and happily with Italian scholars and men of letters and attended meetings of their academies. He followed, perhaps not always strictly, the prudent rule of never introducing religious topics, but, if questioned about his own faith, he concealed nothing. When planning a second visit to Rome he was warned by merchants that English Jesuits there had laid a plot against him; his informants or he himself may have exaggerated the danger, though Protestant travelers in Italy could get into ticklish situations. At any rate Milton was not deterred. The one great man he visited was Galileo, who was living under surveillance outside Florence, "grown old," as Milton recalled in *Areopagitica*, "a prisoner to the Inquisition, for thinking in astronomy otherwise than the Franciscan and Dominican licensers thought."

It is clear from Milton's retrospective sketch in the *Second Defence of the English People* (1654), and from earlier Latin poems and letters to Italian friends, that he enjoyed himself thoroughly and continued to cherish the memory of his tour as a bright spot in his life. Along with the normal pleasures of the cultivated tourist in a richly rewarding country, especially a tourist who settles down and gets to know people and the inside of things, Milton's view of himself must have been agreeably elevated. So far as we can tell, apart from Cambridge acquaintances and Wotton, Milton had no personal connections with English writers—in London he had not been one of Ben

Jonson's tavern coterie—and he had published almost nothing under his name (*Comus* was anonymous and the almost anonymous *Lycidas* was buried in an uninviting anthology), so that his reputation at home was limited to a very small circle. Most of the Italian writers he met are remembered now only because they met him, but the cordial welcome he received as a fellow writer must have done much to fortify his confidence in himself and his vocation. When he published his *Poems* in 1645–1646, there were in the front none of the usual commendatory verses from admirers (though Wotton's letter was prefixed to *Comus*), but the Latin section was headed by testimonies from Italian friends.

In Italy Milton wrote three Latin epigrams in praise of the famous Neapolitan singer Leonora Baroni (who in 1639 received the honor of a volume of *Applausi* from Italian poets), some verses comforting the poet Salzilli in his illness, and one of the best of all his Latin poems, *Mansus*. Giovanni Battista Manso, Marquis of Villa, who showed the young man most cordial attentions in Naples —and said he would have shown more if his guest had been more reticent on religious matters—was an illustrious and venerable figure through having been the patron and biographer of the chief poets of two generations, Tasso and Marino. *Mansus* was more than a bread-and-butter epistle. Much of it was naturally a tribute to Manso's services to letters (the tribute to his still luxuriant hair indicates that his wig was a good one). But the representative of an alien northern muse took occasion, with graceful tact, to apprise Italian complacency that England also had its culture and its poets. In paying compliments to Manso, Milton revealed a new self-confidence and made the first statement of his intention to write an Arthurian epic. At some time during his stay abroad he learned of the death (August, 1638) of Charles Diodati; if he had got the news by this time (December ?, 1638), it might explain the motive and heightened feeling of the conclusion, the poet's wish for a friend like Manso to stand by him in life and death.

Milton had intended to go to Sicily and Greece, but reports from home of increasing disturbance in church and state caused him to give up that idea. However, as he candidly made clear, his return was not hurried. He allowed himself extended second visits in Rome and Florence, made an excursion to Lucca, the home of Diodati's forebears, and spent a month in Venice. From there he shipped home the books he had bought and then journeyed back, by way of Verona, Milan, Lake Leman, Geneva, and France. In Geneva he lingered awhile to talk with Charles's uncle, Giovanni Diodati, a distinguished professor of theology. Milton arrived in England about August 1, after an absence of some fifteen months.

His first piece of writing was an elegy on Diodati, the *Epitaphium Damonis,* which was done in the latter part of 1639 or early in 1640 and privately printed (then or later). While he was abroad Milton probably felt too unsettled to write such a poem; at any rate the impulse became urgent when he found himself again amid the scenes of their intimate association. Diodati, after leaving Oxford, had for a time studied theology at Geneva and then switched to his father's profession, medicine, which he was practicing when he died. The *Epitaphium,* a little longer than *Lycidas,* was not only in the pastoral mode but in Latin, the language of Milton's earlier letters to Diodati in verse and prose, and the poem may well be called, as it has been, his last letter (this time in hexameters). Critics have commonly placed the elegy at the head of Milton's Latin poems, a judgment partly based, one may think, on the feeling that Milton's memorial to his one dear friend ought to rank first. But the poem in itself may be considered by no means a complete success. Perhaps the writer's personal sorrow was too deep and close for such a theme as inspired *Lycidas*; or, on the other hand, possibly the friendship, overlaid by Milton's Italian experience, had receded into the past (the suggestion does not reflect upon the depth of the friendship or the sincerity of the poem). Whatever the cause, Milton elaborates pastoral machinery and much of it remains unvitalized artifice. A few passages are very poignant, passages which directly recall companionship in the fields and beside the winter fire, and which lament the poet's present loneliness, the impossibility of finding another such friend—avowals especially moving from a man so often gratuitously credited with a proud self-sufficiency. But happy memories of Italy, even if they have some logical warrant in Diodati's Italian origins, are tenuously related to him; obtrusive also, despite the apology, is the account of Milton's projected Arthurian epic (which includes his resolve to write it in English, although that means a drastic limiting of his desired audience). In fact, for once the poet does not seem to be in firm control. The concluding vision of Diodati's virgin soul received into heaven is a remarkable blending of the Christian and pagan, even for a Neo-Latinist, but it is strained and hectic, and it does not approach the sublime resolution in *Lycidas* of a central conflict. Whatever be thought of the poem, it marks the end of the first chapter in Milton's life. Henceforth, for twenty years, he was to know the dust and heat of the national arena.

PART THREE

The Revolution and
The Commonwealth

1640–1660

Looking back, in the *Second Defence*, on his situation after his return from Italy, Milton thus summarized the beginning of a new phase in his life:

I, as best I could in such disturbed and fluctuating conditions, looked for a place to live in, and succeeded in renting, for myself and my books, a big enough house in the city. There I took up again with joy my interrupted studies, willing to leave public issues to God first of all, and to those men entrusted by the people with the responsibility.

He was not long willing to remain an innocent bystander. Meanwhile, not being qualified for any profession, he turned to teaching; his first pupils were his small nephews, Edward and John Phillips, and others were added. But there was an occasional frisk (to borrow Dr. Johnson's word). Once in three weeks or a month, says his nephew, Milton

would drop into the society of some young sparks of his acquaintance, the chief whereof were Mr. Alphry and Mr. Miller, two gentlemen of Gray's Inn, the beaux of those times, but nothing near so bad as those nowadays; with these gentlemen he would so far make bold with his body as now and then to keep a gaudy-day.

Yet such diversions, however pleasant to hear of (along with those celebrated in two late sonnets), could be only grace notes to the earnest labors of Milton's life from now on.

Ecclesiastical Tracts

A s *Mansus* and the *Epitaphium Damonis* show, Milton
in 1638–1640 had arrived at the serious Renaissance poet's great ambition, a heroic poem. But growing
conflicts in church and state compelled him to put poetry
aside and join as a pamphleteer in the struggle for liberty.
As time went on, he came to see his defenses of liberty as
at least a partial fulfillment of his frustrated poetic
dreams, a kind of national epic in prose; but when he
began, despite his religious and humanistic sense of the
supreme claims of public duty, it was not easy "to inter-
rupt the pursuit of no less hopes than these, and leave a
calm and pleasing solitariness, fed with cheerful and
confident thoughts, to embark in a troubled sea of noises
and hoarse disputes. . . ."

Milton's mixed feelings may be best depicted by further reference to the personal passage in *The Reason of
Church Government Urged Against Prelaty* (1642), the
fourth of his antiepiscopal tracts. Thinking as usual of his
own perfectionist ideal, he says that, if mere literary
repute were his aim, "I should not write thus out of mine
own season," before completing "the full circle of my
private studies" ("although," he adds, "I complain not of
any insufficiency to the matter in hand"). Moreover,
writing on topics of the moment in tumultuous times, he

cannot linger to produce finished works of art; and, lastly, he is by nature a poet and in this kind of work he has the use but of his left hand. He goes on, as the traditions of rhetoric ordained, to present his credentials, to show his right to speak. In his youth, he reports, his teachers had seen unusual vitality in his writing, especially his verse, and much later, in Italy, he had received such encomiums as Italians rarely bestow on northerners. These outward encouragements were linked with "an inward prompting which now grew daily upon me, that by labor and intent study (which I take to be my portion in this life), joined with the strong propensity of nature, I might perhaps leave something so written to aftertimes as they should not willingly let it die." He sets forth his high conception of poetry and the necessity of deferring the projected heroic poem—the taking of his mainly non-literary Presbyterian readers into his confidence is typical of Milton's sublime naïveté—and then returns to the paramount duty of trying

to help ease and lighten the difficult labors of the church, to whose service, by the intentions of my parents and friends, I was destined of a child and in mine own resolutions, till coming to some maturity of years and perceiving what tyranny had invaded the church—that he who would take orders must subscribe slave and take an oath withal, which, unless he took with a conscience that would retch, he must either straight perjure or split his faith—I thought it better to prefer a blameless silence before the sacred office of speaking, bought and begun with servitude and forswearing. Howsoever thus church-outed by the prelates, hence may appear the right I have to meddle in these matters, as before the necessity and constraint appeared.

Although by the middle of the century Puritanism had developed many inner complexities and variations, which were manifested in splinter groups large and small, the essential motive and the earlier history of the movement were simple and logical. The Church of England as established by the Elizabethan settlement, coming after the rapid succession of changes under Henry VIII, Edward VI, and Mary, had to be a broad-based compromise if it was to be a national church and gather in all but extreme and unreconcilable Catholics and Protestants. Hence the church retained the traditional hierarchy and much of the traditional liturgy (this now in the beautiful English of Cranmer's *Book of Common Prayer*), while of course it substituted Protestant for Romanist doctrines wherever these clashed. But the retention of the hierarchy and the liturgy was opposed by ultra-Protestants, who demanded, not a compromise, but a purgation. Their ideal was the democratic and nonliturgical simplicity of the apostolic church as they saw it in the New Testament. This is the core of the matter in Milton's first tract of 1641, as it had been during the previous eighty years, years punctuated by Puritan agitation. The apostolic ideal—which appeared both nebulous and irrational to philosophic churchmen like Richard Hooker—had been realized, after a fashion, in John Knox's Scottish Kirk, and, up into the 1640's, the main body of English Puritans may be called Presbyterian in fact or in sympathy. During the Elizabethan age most Puritans were content to be a left wing within the church, but, beginning with Robert Browne and the Brownists in the 1580's, and especially after 1600, various groups split off in various directions. It is important to remember that, until well on in the seventeenth century, there was no theological division: the orthodox clergy and laity of the church were Calvinist in belief like the Puritan opposition. Thus King James, not only the official head of the church but a learned theologian, was a staunch Calvinist who abhorred Puritanism. And Milton's decision against becoming a clergyman did not spring from his Calvinist beliefs but, as we have just seen, from his dislike of episcopal tyranny—and his devotion to poetry.

In the sixteenth and seventeenth centuries religion and politics were so inextricably interwoven that the briefest summary of either takes in the other. At the Hampton Court Conference of 1604 King James brusquely stated his policy, "No bishop, no king," and declared that he would make Puritans conform or else harry them out of the land. About ninety Puritan clergymen were soon ejected from their livings. Some people moved to Holland; and in 1620 the *Mayflower* carried its band of pilgrims to what Milton in his first tract called "the savage deserts of America." In 1633 the elevation of Bishop Laud to the archbishopric of Canterbury inaugurated a program of much sterner repression. Since the very survival of the national church was in danger, Laud, with worthy motives but with unimaginative, inflexible, and sometimes brutal severity, used every means to subdue nonconformity and promote unity: to Puritans his motto seemed to be "The spirit killeth, but the letter giveth life." In addition to metropolitan "visitations," Laud worked through the courts of Star Chamber and High Commission, so that these institutions became bywords for arbitrary tyranny. The efforts of King Charles and Laud to impose episcopacy upon Scotland (efforts begun by King James) led to the Scottish National Covenant of 1638 and the futile and half-farcical Bishops' Wars of 1639 and 1640. In the spring of 1640, after eleven years without a parliament, Charles was forced by need of money to summon one, but it proved refractory. The Convocation of the church, which met at the same time, promulgated Laudian Canons hateful to Puritans. November of 1640 brought the first meeting of what was to be the Long Parliament, since through various vicissitudes it lasted until 1660.

The years of Charles's personal rule had seen some particular reforms, as in the relief of the poor, yet such rule was none the less absolutism and it abundantly nourished all the old grievances, political, economic, and religious. The close alliance between crown and church cemented the alliance between parliament and Puritanism, and seething discontent boiled over in the first sessions of the Long Parliament. It attacked the Earl of Strafford, Laud's political counterpart, and Laud himself, and executed the former in 1641, the latter in 1645. It affirmed the illegality of ship-money and the Canons issued by the church Convocation, and it abolished the hated Star Chamber and Court of High Commission. One early and vociferous battle cry was the Root and Branch Petition of December, 1640—signed, it was said, by 15,000 Londoners—which demanded the abolition of episcopacy "with all its dependencies, roots and branches."

In the early months of 1640 Joseph Hall, who had begun his career as an Elizabethan satirist and was now a moderate bishop, had published *Episcopacy by Divine Right Asserted*, and in January, 1641, he followed it up with *An Humble Remonstrance to the High Court of Parliament*. Hall was soon answered by a group of Presbyterian divines whose initials made up the collective name of Smectymnuus (the "ty" stood for Milton's old tutor, Thomas Young). Hall replied with *A Defence of the Humble Remonstrance* (probably April, 1641). Milton joined battle, on the Presbyterian side, with *Of Reformation Touching Church Discipline in England*, published probably in May, 1641. His four other anti-episcopal tracts were: *Of Prelatical Episcopacy* (June–July, 1641), a reply especially to Hall and a tract by the noted scholar James Ussher, Archbishop of Armagh; *Animadversions upon the Remonstrant's Defence against Smectymnuus* (probably July, 1641), against Hall; *The Reason of Church Government Urged against Prelaty*

(January–February, 1642), a reply to a collection of old
and recent tracts by Andrewes, Ussher, and others; and,
finally, what is known by an abridged title as *An Apology
for Smectymnuus* (April, 1642), a rejoinder to an attack
(by Hall and his son?) on Milton's *Animadversions* and
his personal character. His defensive account of his early
idealism in the *Apology* was partly quoted in connection
with *Comus,* and the personal passage in the *Reason of
Church Government* has also been cited and will be
again. The *Reason*—which alone carried Milton's name—
is the most temperate and rational (and biblical) of his
five tracts, but the first one, *Of Reformation*, has points
of general and special interest.

Milton's position is that already indicated as the aim of
Puritanism: he seeks the completing of the Reformation,
the restoring of the apostolic church in its primitive simplicity and purity. The first step is the abolition of those
feudal potentates, the bishops, and of Anglican ritualism,
"the new-vomited paganism of sensual idolatry." Such
phrases give us a shock when we recall the description
of an Anglican service in *Il Penseroso*; but they and much
else go with the Puritan contrast between external forms
and the religion of the spirit. The central Reformation
doctrines of the priesthood of all believers, individual
responsibility to God, and the unique authority of Scripture in all matters of belief and conduct and church
discipline, inspire not only attacks on episcopal tradition
but idealistic visions of the holy society, of the spiritual
enlightenment given to the humblest reader of the Bible.

Milton feels patriotic pride in his country's having
been, through Wycliffe, the pioneer of the Reformation.
The reading done at Horton in history and in the church
fathers bears fruit, sometimes prickly fruit, in his survey
of the European, English, and ecclesiastical past. The
cultivated man of letters—who is rarely visible in the
multitudinous controversial pamphlets of the age—shows

himself in quotations from Dante, Petrarch, Ariosto, Chaucer, and a satire supposed to be Chaucer's, *The Plowman's Tale*. At this time the future republican is an unquestioning monarchist, concerned to show that episcopacy "is not only not agreeable, but tending to the destruction of monarchy." At this time Milton is also an orthodox Trinitarian. The tract bursts at the end into a grandly Miltonic prayer. He appeals for the preservation of the expiring church and the shaken monarchy, recalls the invasions and perils England has survived down to the scattering of the Spanish Armada, and looks exultantly for the second coming of Christ, "the eternal and shortly expected King," who will end all earthly tyrannies and inaugurate a new era of joy and bliss, distributing rewards to those who "have been earnest for the common good of religion and their country." For himself Milton sees a more special role: "Then, amidst the hymns and halleluiahs of saints, some one may perhaps be heard offering at high strains in new and lofty measures to sing and celebrate thy divine mercies and marvelous judgments in this land throughout all ages. . . ." The final sentence, a paragraph, is an also Miltonic curse, a prayer —more ample and precise than the prophecy of "that two-handed engine at the door"—that the bishops "after a shameful end in this life (which God grant them), shall be thrown down eternally into the darkest and deepest gulf of hell. . . ."

We naturally wish that Milton's vision of a people animated by a pure spirituality had carried with it less bitter violence against bishops in general and Hall in particular (Ussher he treated with respect). But we may try to understand, without excusing, his polemical motives and methods, although many modern readers have small sympathy with men of the past for whom the religious welfare of souls here and hereafter was the one supreme concern. In Milton the expression of that concern was heightened by a tendency, found sometimes even in cloistered scholars, to see opponents not as persons with principles and feelings but as enemies of a sacred cause who must be annihilated with every weapon in the arsenal of rhetoric; and for him even more than for other men of the age there was sacred precedent for invective in the Hebrew prophets and the Psalmist. Also, Milton, in his early thirties, was conducting his education in public; at first, dreaming of a better world, he embraced antiprelacy as many young modern idealists embraced Communism, and when he discovered, in a couple of years, that Presbyterianism was not Utopia, he said so, very forcefully. Then, too, Milton is often singled out as the great or the only culprit by writers who do not know or choose to forget the controversial violence of such earlier churchmen as Bishop Andrewes and Dr. Donne.

Marriage and Tracts on Divorce

A T THE END of May or beginning of June, 1642, Milton married. In the words of Edward Phillips,

About Whitsuntide it was, or a little after, that he took a journey into the country, nobody about him certainly knowing the reason, or that it was any more than a journey of recreation. After a month's stay, home he returns a married man, that went out a bachelor, his wife being Mary, the eldest daughter of Mr. Richard Powell, then a justice of peace, of Forest Hill, near Shotover in Oxfordshire.

Milton was thirty-three. Mary Powell was seventeen; no doubt she was pretty and no doubt she had had the very limited education commonly given to daughters of even the well-to-do, since they were expected to marry early and be capable household managers and prolific mothers. The results of such a marriage might have been predicted by anyone except Milton. To quote Phillips again (and skip his account of several days' feasting of the bride's relatives and friends at the house of the bridegroom, whose jollity may have waned):

By that time she had for a month or thereabout led a philosophical life (after having been used to a great house and much company and joviality), her friends, possibly incited by her own desire, made earnest suit by letter to have her company the remaining part of the summer, which was granted,

on condition of her returning at the time appointed, Michaelmas or thereabout. . . .

Michaelmas being come, and no news of his wife's return,
he sent for her by letter; and receiving no answer, sent
several other letters, which were also unanswered; so that at
last he dispatched down a foot messenger with a letter,
desiring her return. But the messenger came back not only
without an answer, at least a satisfactory one, but, to the best
of my remembrance, reported that he was dismissed with
some sort of contempt. This proceeding, in all probability,
was grounded upon no other cause but this, namely, that the
family being generally addicted to the cavalier party, as they
called it, and some of them possibly engaged in the King's
service, who by this time had his headquarters at Oxford,
and was in some prospect of success, they began to repent
them of having matched the eldest daughter of the family
to a person so contrary to them in opinion; and thought it
would be a blot in their escutcheon, whenever that court
should come to flourish again.

The prolonging of the visit into separation may, as
Phillips says (and as Milton may imply in remarks on
his divorce tracts in the *Second Defence*), have been due
or partly due to opposed sympathies in regard to the
civil war, which had begun on August 22, 1642. The
probable personal factors in the rift are more obvious
than Milton's motives in his choice of a wife. The scholar-
poet may have decided on general principles that, being
now settled in his life's work, he should marry, and his
acquaintance with young women may have been small;
he may have known or known of the Powells mainly
because Richard Powell owed his father money. Whatever the external facts, we may be sure—as a quotation
below suggests—that he had taken the momentous step
not only seriously but prayerfully, even if he lacked
psychological and worldly wisdom. And he may have
been somewhat deceived by his senses. At any rate
Milton experienced the shock of recognizing that he,

who had sought in all things to live as in his great Task-Master's eye, had made his first mistake, an irreparable mistake, one that affected the roots of his being and the whole course of his daily life and work.

Milton was now impelled to carry his campaign for freedom into territory where he would find no allies, only united opposition. *The Doctrine and Discipline of Divorce* was published anonymously about August 1, 1643; a much enlarged edition, with the author's name, appeared in January or February, 1644. *The Judgment of Martin Bucer concerning Divorce* (August, 1644) was a condensed translation from an eminent Reformation divine whose views, Milton had just discovered, anticipated his own and could not be so readily condemned. *Tetrachordon*, an exposition of the four biblical *loci classici*, and *Colasterion*, a reply to an attack on the *Doctrine and Discipline*, were both published in March, 1645. The first and third tracts are the most important, and we may look chiefly at the first.

While Milton argued for divorce as a private and not a public matter and for the right of both parties to remarry, his main thesis, driven home in many ways from many angles, was that adultery, the accepted cause for divorce, is less grievous than the continued effects of incompatibility of mind and temper, which poisons the very essence of marriage. At intervals we seem to hear the voice of anguished experience:

The soberest and best governed men are least practised in these affairs; and who knows not that the bashful muteness of a virgin may ofttimes hide all the unliveliness and natural sloth which is really unfit for conversation?* . . . And lastly, it is not strange though many, who have spent their youth chastely, are in some things not so quick-sighted, while they haste too eagerly to light the nuptial torch. . . .

* In English of the period, "conversation" has the broad meanings of intellectual and moral character and behavior.

And yet there follows upon this a worse temptation: for if
he be such as hath spent his youth unblamably, and laid up
his chiefest earthly comforts in the enjoyment of a contented
marriage, nor did neglect that furtherance which was to be
obtained therein by constant prayers; when he shall find
himself bound fast to an uncomplying discord of nature, or,
as it oft happens, to an image of earth and phlegm, with
whom he looked to be the copartner of a sweet and gladsome
society, and sees withal that his bondage is now inevita-
ble; though he be almost the strongest Christian, he will
be ready to despair in virtue, and mutiny against Divine
Providence. . . .

But if his own situation was the immediate stimulus
for his tracts, Milton's arguments had a broad base, which
grew broader as he went on. The subject of marriage
had been of concern to church fathers and Reformation
divines, as Milton amply showed; his own previous concern with it is indicated by the anonymous biographer
and by entries, mostly of 1640–1644 and some earlier,
in his Commonplace Book. Even if he had been happily
married, or not married at all, he would probably have
got around in time to a question so important and so
much discussed. Like all other people, he assumed the
superior status of men in the chain of being (women
being what they commonly were in intellectual cultivation, general experience supported theory), but he was
seeking "the good of both sexes" and he shared a high
and especially Puritan and humanistic ideal of love and
marriage. Whereas the law respected only the body, a
true marriage is of the mind and heart, the fulfilling of
conjugal love and helpfulness. Milton did not see a wife
as a remedy against burning (the Pauline view reiterated
in the sermons of that notable lover, John Donne), or as
a domestic manager or as a breeder of heirs, but as a
genuine companion and solace. And in exalting the husband Milton exalted the wife who was to be a loving

and beloved helpmate: "love in marriage cannot live nor subsist unless it be mutual." But the forced continuance of a loveless union "is a heinous barbarism both against the honor of marriage, the dignity of man and his soul, the goodness of Christianity, and all the human respects of civility"; and "honest liberty is the greatest foe to dishonest license."

When in the *Second Defence* (1654) Milton looked back on his pamphleteering, he saw himself, the bishops disposed of, turning his

thoughts elsewhere, to see if I could in any way promote the cause of real and substantial liberty—which is to be sought from within and not from without, and is to be gained, not through fighting, but rather through right principles and right conduct. I perceived that there are three main kinds of liberty essential to a satisfying mode of life, religious, domestic or private, and civil; and, since I had already written on the first, and saw that the magistrates were actively forwarding the third, I took as my province the second or domestic kind of liberty. But this also seemed to involve three problems, the true conception of marriage, the sound education of children, and freedom of thought and speech. . . .

In retrospect Milton's efforts took a more systematic shape than they had in fact taken, since they had been partly occasioned by circumstances; yet such circumstances encouraged discussion of problems to which he had already given more or less thought. The pamphlets on various topics are related and do show his evolving principles, along with some radical changes in opinion and alignment.

In the address to parliament and the Westminster Assembly with which Milton opened the second edition of the *Doctrine and Discipline of Divorce*, he took the reforming of marriage laws as part of the great revolution now going on. If his tracts were ineffectual, his thinking was significant. In wrestling with biblical pronouncements on divorce, as he was bound to do, and in wresting them to fit his own liberal views, he can be seen moving toward two great principles—already adumbrated in the *Reason of Church Government*—which could coalesce and fortify each other. One was "Christian liberty," a heritage from Luther and Calvin which was extended and widely utilized in the Puritan revolution, and which, in its fullest development, emancipated the individual Christian conscience from both the Mosaic law and any modern civil or religious authority. The other was the Christianized Stoic doctrine of "right reason," the moral faculty implanted in all men alike, what Hooker called "the general and perpetual voice of men"; this, in Hooker's words, "is as the sentence of God himself" because it constitutes the law of nature which has universal validity and which God himself could not alter. The two principles—two kinds of inner light—might be said to come together, in summary form, in Milton's assertion in *Tetrachordon* that "no ordinance, human or from heaven, can bind against the good of man." Such a position—and the rational freedom demanded in *Areopagitica*—may at first sight seem anomalous in a Calvinist, but Milton was still a Calvinist in 1644–1645, as he indicates in his references to Arminius in the *Doctrine and Discipline* (II.iii) and *Areopagitica*. The fact is a wholesome reminder that Calvinism could operate in more ways than popular modern notions would allow.

Milton's mostly anonymous pamphlets against the bishops had been part of a general controversy, but now, despite the turmoil of civil war, he received his first real recognition, as a disreputable libertine. In a sermon to parliament in February, 1644, his old tutor, Thomas Young, perhaps administered a veiled rebuke, and in August another Presbyterian divine, Herbert Palmer, censured him in another parliamentary sermon. The House of Commons, in response to an appeal from the

Stationers' Company, instructed a committee "diligently to inquire out the authors, printers, and publishers of the pamphlet against the immortality of the soul [by Richard Overton], and concerning divorce." William Prynne, the Presbyterian pamphleteer, urged the suppression of these and other wicked books. In December the Stationers' Company complained to the House of Lords about the "printing of scandalous books by divers, as Hezekiah Woodward and John Milton." Milton's early anonymous biographer gives this report:

The Assembly of Divines then sitting at Westminster, though formerly obliged by his learned pen in the defense of Smectymnuus and other of their controversies with the bishops, now impatient of having the clergy's jurisdiction, as they reckoned it, invaded, instead of answering or disproving what those books had asserted, caused him to be summoned for them before the Lords. But that house, whether approving the doctrine or not favoring his accusers, soon dismissed him.

The Anglican cleric, Daniel Featley, also denounced the tracts; and the royalist layman and man of the world, James Howell, author of the lively *Epistolae Ho-elianae*, referred to Milton as "a poor shallow-brained puppy." The main attacks, however, came from Milton's quondam allies and helped to complete a disillusionment with Presbyterianism that he was already feeling on broader grounds; his general and particular reactions were forcefully expressed in *Areopagitica* and several sonnets.

Of Education

THE SHORT PAMPHLET *Of Education* was published
anonymously about June 4–5, 1644, some two
months before the second tract on divorce. Perhaps because it was the first innocuous piece Milton had written,
it was the first to be regularly entered with and licensed
by the Stationers' Company. Samuel Hartlib, to whom it
was addressed, was a new type of public-spirited citizen
who devoted himself to all kinds of progressive enter-
prises, perhaps chiefly the advancement of science and
educational reform. He was a zealous follower of the
famous Czech educator, John Amos Comenius, whose
ultimate ideal of religious unity and world peace included a large concern with universal, compulsory, ele-
mentary, and practical education; he might be called a
sort of religious John Dewey. Hartlib had been translating and publishing Comenius' educational writings
and he had been the main agent in bringing their author
to England in 1641–1642 to establish a Baconian "pan-
sophic" college—a project which parliament, occupied
with the Irish rising and other affairs, failed to support.
Hartlib, after talk with Milton, had asked him, as he
asked other men, to set down his thoughts on education;
but agreement on some points of method may have misled both men into assuming agreement on fundamental

aims, and much of Milton's tract could hardly have been welcome to a thoroughgoing modernist.

Milton began with compliments on Hartlib's general repute and his promotion of good causes, but then dismissed the "many modern *Januas* and *Didactics*" (Comenius' books) and proceeded with a discourse which may be called the last of the line of treatises on education written by European humanists since the early fifteenth century. Like his great predecessors, Erasmus, Budé, Vives, and others, Milton was adapting the classical program to the needs of a modern Christian country. The traditional object, "virtue and good letters," meant the education of the ruling class—understood in a broad sense—for the active and intelligent exercise of civic responsibility. (Milton was later to be more concerned about popular education.) One of his two definitions is much less often quoted than the other, but is more central and comprehensive:

The end then of learning is to repair the ruins of our first parents by regaining to know God aright, and out of that knowledge to love him, to imitate him, to be like him, as we may the nearest by possessing our souls of true virtue, which, being united to the heavenly grace of faith, makes up the highest perfection.

There, very explicitly, is the lifelong vision of fall and recovery that inspired Milton's prose and poetry. The more familiar definition stresses the humanistic aim:

I call therefore a complete and generous education that which fits a man to perform justly, skilfully, and magnanimously all the offices, both private and public, of peace and war.

Milton was of course writing in wartime and took account of the practical exigencies of war; in the late major poems he was a vehement antimilitarist.

Milton could, independently, share the Comenian hos-

tility to gerund-grinding and insist on the rapid acquisi-
tion of languages as tools; he shared also the Comenian
principle of a gradual advance from simple sensory
experience to higher levels; and—unlike most of the
earlier humanists, except Rabelais—he was enough of a
Baconian to give large importance to all branches of
science. But otherwise Milton's ideal of education was far
removed from that of Comenius and his English disciples,
who had no use for literary and imaginative culture and
urged a narrow and illiberal vocationalism, with a common—and rudimentary—core of scientific and religious
knowledge. For Milton, Greek and Latin (with Italian
and Hebrew added) are the literature of both knowledge
and power, in all areas from agriculture to law, from
comedy to political thought, from the principles of rhetoric and literary criticism to ethical judgment (ethics
being always subject to "the determinate sentence" of
the Bible). The doctrine of "imitation" had often been
taken, in and since antiquity, as shallow formalism, and
it was to be still oftener in the century after Milton, but
in education it has for him, as for some earlier humanists,
its simplest and most authentic meaning:

When all these employments are well conquered, then will
the choice histories, heroic poems, and Attic tragedies of
stateliest and most regal argument, with all the famous political orations, offer themselves; which, if they were not only
read, but some of them got by memory, and solemnly pronounced with right accent and grace, as might be taught,
would endue them even with the spirit and vigor of Demos-
thenes or Cicero, Euripides or Sophocles.

Milton's academy—apart from the Christian framework
of the program—is professedly like the schools of Greece
"out of which were bred up such a number of renowned
philosophers, orators, historians, poets, and princes all
over Greece, Italy, and Asia. . . ." In short, its dynamic

spirit is (to borrow Whitehead's phrase) the habitual vision of greatness.

All this was alien to the modernist Puritan and Comenian combination of practical training and practical piety. Comenian ideas, whether or not derived from Comenius, appealed strongly to various kinds of Puritans who disliked traditional education as pagan, aristocratic, and useless. Not to mention lesser men, William Petty (later to be known as the founder of political economy) responded to a request from Hartlib with a hardheaded tract on "real learning," that is, practical science. No doubt the Comenian plan had something to be said for it, on its own drab and stuffy level. But Milton was concerned with education, with individual cultivation and growth and public responsibility. His ideal academy, which was to be the prototype of many, would take care of boys from the age of twelve to twenty-one; it would therefore replace both secondary school and the preprofessional years of the university. In some positive and negative ways—as in getting rid of a useless and premature emphasis on logic, which he had resented at Cambridge—Milton was, so to speak, carrying on the spirit and lengthening the curriculum of St. Paul's School. According to Edward Phillips, one of his first pupils, Milton followed much the same principles and recommended texts in his own teaching. American readers, by the way, and perhaps others as well, often recoil from Milton's heavy requirements, but these should be compared with the standards of the age and not with ours; Renaissance humanists did not believe in adjustment to life through the prolonging of infancy.

◆◀◆◀◆◀◆ **4** ◗◆◗◆◗◆

Areopagitica

IN NOVEMBER, 1644, five months after *Of Education,*
Milton published his greatest piece of English prose
and one of the great possessions of the race, *Areopagitica.*
But if the tract is in one sense timeless, its strategy and
much of its substance were conditioned by immediate
circumstances. During 1644 the predominant theme of
controversy had been religious toleration. In *Areopagitica*
Milton treated that problem most directly in a general
plea for mutual charity and unity of spirit in the bond
of peace; but its presence is felt throughout. In July,
1643, the Westminster Assembly, composed of divines
and some laymen, met under parliamentary auspices to
reorganize the Church of England, presumably on the
Presbyterian model. The expected unanimity, however,
struck a snag. Five sober ministers, who had held pastor-
ates abroad and had some special prestige as exiles,
asked permission to continue with independent but non-
separating congregations. Failing to soften Presbyterian
rigidity in the Assembly, they carried debate into the parliamentary and public domain by publishing *An Apolo-
getical Narration* (January, 1644). The particular issue
rapidly widened into the general problem of toleration.
In *Queries of Highest Consideration* (February), the
radical Roger Williams argued against any kind of reli-

gious compulsion. In March, Henry Robinson, a man of
business, supported religious liberty mainly for the sake
of peace and prosperity. A more cultivated lover of peace
and a hater of clerical dissension, the Leveller William
Walwyn, made in June or July his third plea for comprehensive toleration (*The Compassionate Samaritan*). In
July came Williams's famous *Bloody Tenent of Persecu-
tion*, in which, developing his earlier argument, he demanded complete separation of church and state and
complete freedom of conscience. In October the noted
Independent preacher, John Goodwin, published his
philosophic *Theomachia*. All along there were defenses
of Presbyterian uniformity from Scotsmen and the tireless
William Prynne and others. Thus, although such men
as Robinson and Walwyn urged freedom of the press,
Areopagitica, appearing in November, was not quite in
the main line of current debate; Milton was of course
on the libertarian side, though he did not go so far as
Williams. He registered his thorough hostility to the
Presbyterians, who had championed freedom until they
themselves gained power but now were no less tyrannical
than the bishops had been. From this controversy—
which did not end in 1644—the Independents, for whom
toleration was an initial necessity for survival, emerged
as the liberal body of Puritans, between the reactionary
Presbyterians on the right and the multiplying groups
and sects of radicals on the left. Milton found Independency congenial, at least until he moved into his final
independence.

Milton's central theme had its background also. Censorship of books had operated in England since the early
fifteenth century and was authorized by the Tudor sov-
ereigns from Henry VIII onward (Milton identified it
with papal decrees and the Council of Trent and the
Spanish Inquisition). After 1566 it was bound up with
the process of publishing under the authority of the

Stationers' Company, the association or guild of printers and publishers which controlled or tried to control all questions relating to their business. In Shakespeare's time and later, books had to be entered in the records of the Company and approved by the Archbishop of Canterbury or the Bishop of London (in practice, by their chaplains or a panel of censors); the publication of plays came under the jurisdiction of the Master of the Revels. Censorship was strongly reinforced by a Star Chamber decree of 1637. But increasingly vocal concern with problems of church and state, and the Long Parliament's abolition of the Star Chamber in 1641, let loose a flood of unlicensed pamphlets, Milton's among them. In June, 1643, after several provisional attempts at restraint, parliament put forth an ordinance—the one Milton quotes and takes as his text—which was, as he says, virtually a revival of the Star Chamber decree. Milton's grand protest was doubtless somewhat belated, but he had been preoccupied with his first two tracts on divorce (and the enlarging of the first one) and *Of Education*. Also, it may have taken a while to measure the seriousness of the renewal of censorship by a parliament supposedly committed to forwarding the cause of liberty; the policy of the Westminster Assembly had become clear during the autumn of 1643. *Areopagitica* seems to have been written with more care than most of Milton's previous tracts, and he was tactful in addressing parliament and praising its achievements; yet these made all the more regrettable such backsliding on so great a matter as freedom of the press. It may be added that, except for a short time later, the press was under official controls throughout the revolution.

Milton's title had reference to the speech written by Isocrates and addressed to the Athenian assembly, on enlarging the powers of the old court of the Areopagus, and his discourse was modeled on a classical oration. His argument develops four main points. The first is that censorship, in its modern form, is a product of the Catholic Inquisition and hence should be odious to Protestant England. The second, "what is to be thought in general of reading, whatever sort the books be," evokes from a scholar-poet the most eloquent defense of promiscuous reading and the exercise of the individual's God-given reason and discrimination. The second and third points are

that this order avails nothing to the suppressing of scandalous, seditious, and libelous books, which were mainly intended to be suppressed; last, that it will be primely to the discouragement of all learning, and the stop of truth, not only by disexercising and blunting our abilities in what we know already, but by hindering and cropping the discovery that might be yet further made both in religious and civil wisdom.

Areopagitica has often been loosely cited as a plea for complete freedom of speech, which it is not. The most liberal seventeenth-century mind would endorse the modern dictum that no one has the right to shout "Fire!" in a crowded theater, and would insist, as Milton does, on safeguards for religious, moral, and political security. So, while denouncing with all his might the censorship of books before publication, he explicitly accepts the necessity of judicious censorship of published books. In the broader area of toleration, he excludes "popery and open superstition" (a political as well as religious danger) and "that also which is impious or evil absolutely, either against faith or manners." Apart from these reservations, Milton expresses unbounded confidence in progressive enlightenment through free discussion, in the power of truth to win its way against error, and in the special capacity of his countrymen—whom he celebrates once more as the pioneers of Protestantism—to create a new society, a new world. Faith in Providence and history answer the question that when, as now,

God is decreeing to begin some new and great period in his church, even to the reforming of reformation itself, what does he then but reveal himself to his servants and, as his manner is, first to his Englishmen? . . . Behold now this vast city, a city of refuge, the mansion-house of liberty, encompassed and surrounded with his protection. . . .

God is again leading his chosen people out of Egypt to the promised land.

Methinks I see in my mind a noble and puissant nation rousing herself like a strong man after sleep, and shaking her invincible locks: methinks I see her as an eagle mewing* her mighty youth, and kindling her undazzled eyes at the full midday beam, purging and unscaling her long-abused sight at the fountain itself of heavenly radiance. . . .

In general, Milton insists that people cannot be legislated into goodness and must not be molded into a starched conformity. In tones that range from satire to sublimity he asserts the Platonic and Christian principle that righteousness is a matter of inward discipline and growth, that in a world of good and evil man must exercise the power of moral choice, that the condition of freedom is freedom to err. The most beautiful and famous sentence in all his prose is signally Miltonic in substance:

I cannot praise a fugitive and cloistered virtue, unexercised and unbreathed, that never sallies out and sees her adversary, but slinks out of the race where that immortal garland is to be run for, not without dust and heat.

What is nowadays the best-known of the countless seventeenth-century pamphlets was almost ignored in its own time. Milton's history of censorship was apparently utilized in 1645 by the Levellers John Lilburne and Richard Overton, and there were incidental echoes elsewhere, but none of the few references shows any aware-

* Renewing (through molting).

ness that a great voice had delivered a classic utterance. The fact invites a word or two about Milton's general capacity as a publicist and the qualities of his style. For us, even if he had never written a line of poetry, his prose works would remain an important statement of the aims and motives of the Puritan revolution; he might, with qualifications, be called the Bacon of the movement. Of economic matters he knew and said little; but most of the other and—it may be thought—more central issues he did treat, and with disinterested zeal for the achievement of both freedom and righteousness. His writings are commonly and justly considered to have had small influence on opinions, still less on events, in their own day, although influence is hard to measure. Our chief guide is the body of allusions and echoes in print, and in the 1640's the larger portion of these had to do with Milton's views on divorce; but in general, in all ages, friendly readers are much less given to expressing their sentiments than enemies. So far as Milton failed to catch the public ear, some reasons would be the "unrealistic" fervor of his idealism, the amount of historical and exegetical learning his pamphlets carried, and his lack, except at moments, of the journalistic skills that popular controversy developed, notably in the Levellers and in the editors of now multiplying newspapers. On the other hand, Milton's libertarian ideas were decidedly alive from the later seventeenth century onward. At any rate, if Miltonic qualities worked against Milton in his own time, they may enhance his value for modern students; he puts his subjects in a large perspective.

Areopagitica displays the full range of Milton's powers in prose. Examples of impetuous and exalted eloquence have been quoted, eloquence that is none the less moving because the author seems to be communing with himself rather than his readers. Both on that high level, as the quotations show, and on the lower level of satire, visual

images and metaphors abound: Catholic imprimaturs
are seen on title pages "complimenting and ducking
each to other with their shaven reverences"; people are
thought so unprincipled "that the whiff of every new
pamphlet should stagger them out of their catechism
and Christian walking." There are, further, such passages
of extended irony as that on the licensing of music,
dancing, eating, and drinking, or the "character" of the
prosperous businessman who takes his religion on trust
from his minister. But Milton's name is identified with
impassioned elevation, a label that covers most of
Areopagitica, and, while much of his prose is now of
interest only to literary and historical scholars, one never
knows in what unpromising context one may come on a
sudden jet of prophetic utterance—for example, the
casual, parenthetical phrase, "that as no man apprehends
what vice is so well as he who is truly virtuous, no man
knows hell like him who converses most in heaven"
(*Doctrine and Discipline of Divorce*, II.xvii). It is often
said that the most severely disciplined of English poets
wrote the most exuberantly undisciplined prose, though
Milton's sentences should not daunt a generation that has
assimilated William Faulkner's. Whether lofty, "mean,"
or lowly, Milton's prose suggests the speaking voice; and
it nourished some of the characteristics of diction,
imagery, and syntax, and the tough muscular fiber, that
belong to the style of *Paradise Lost*. Historically, Milton's
prose is in the Ciceronian tradition, though the hastier
his writing the looser the accumulation of clauses and
phrases that crowd into his mind. He stands apart from
the main line of conscious stylists of the earlier seventeenth century, who more or less cultivated Senecan
prose, informally relaxed or clipped and pointed, and
avoided the rotund oratorical amplitude of the Ciceronian
period; in fact Milton gibed at the short sentences of the
notably Senecan Joseph Hall.

Mrs. Milton; *Poems; History of Britain*

IT MAY HAVE BEEN in 1645 that, according to Edward Phillips, Milton—perhaps anticipating the biblical sanction of polygamy which he later included in his *Christian Doctrine*—conceived "a design of marrying one of Dr. Davis's daughters, a very handsome and witty gentlewoman, but averse, as it is said, to this motion." "However," Phillips proceeded,

the intelligence hereof, and the then declining state of the King's cause, and consequently of the circumstances of Justice Powell's family, caused them to set all engines on work to restore the late married woman to the station wherein they a little before had planted her. At last this device was pitched upon. There dwelt in the lane of St. Martin's-le-Grand, which was hard by, a relation of our author's, one Blackborough, whom it was known he often visited, and upon this occasion the visits were the more narrowly observed, and possibly there might be a combination between both parties, the friends on both sides concentring in the same action, though on different behalfs. One time above the rest, he making his usual visit, the wife was ready in another room, and on a sudden he was surprised to see one whom he thought to have never seen more, making submission and begging pardon on her knees before him. He might probably at first make some show of aversion and rejection; but partly his own generous nature, more inclinable to reconciliation than to

perseverance in anger and revenge, and partly the strong inter-
cession of friends on both sides, soon brought him to an act
of oblivion and a firm league of peace for the future; and it
was at length concluded that she should remain at a friend's
house till such time as he was settled in his new house at
Barbican and all things for her reception in order. . . .

This circumstantial narrative, though it was written
long after the event and included some conjecture, is
presumably true in essentials and may be in details. The
reconciliation certainly took place in 1645. Milton soon
gave proof of magnanimity in a way that was torment for
a scholar, teacher, and writer: when in the summer of
1646, after the fall of Oxford, the Powells lost their estate,
he took them in—his wife's "father and mother," says
Phillips, "and several of her brothers and sisters, which
were in all pretty numerous." The Powell invasion lasted
nearly a year. In a letter of April 21, 1647, to his Italian
friend Carlo Dati, Milton burst out with a cry of pain
about his "in-laws" and other uncongenial persons who,
whenever they felt inclined, sat daily in his company
and bored and vexed him to death, while he was almost
cut off from his real friends by either their death or their
remoteness. His father-in-law, Richard Powell, died on
January 1, 1647. His own father, who had been living
with him since April, 1643, died on or about March 13,
1647; later in the year Milton gave up most of his pupils
and moved to a smaller house.

At the beginning of January, 1646, appeared *Poems of
Mr. John Milton, both English and Latin, Compos'd at
several times* (the edition is commonly cited according
to the Old Style date on the title page, 1645). The witless
portrait of Milton by the chief London engraver, William
Marshall, did not please its subject, and he wrote a Greek
quatrain on the artist's lack of skill which the Greekless
Marshall duly engraved below. The publisher Humphrey
Moseley, the most literary member of his tribe, inserted

a preface in which he praised "as true a birth as the Muses have brought forth since our famous Spenser wrote; whose poems in these English ones are as rarely imitated as sweetly excelled." The praise was none the less sound and sincere for including a reference to another volume Moseley had published in 1645, "Mr. Waller's late choice pieces." As we noted earlier, the Latin section included eulogies Milton had received from Italian friends, and his own deprecation of their extravagance. To the text of *Comus* was prefixed the letter of advice on travel which Sir Henry Wotton had written to Milton on April 13, 1638, the letter containing praise of the masque:

Wherein I should much commend the tragical part, if the lyrical did not ravish me with a certain Doric delicacy in your songs and odes, whereunto I must plainly confess to have seen yet nothing parallel in our language: *ipsa mollities.*

Sir Henry, it may be remembered, was himself the author of two famous lyrics, *The Character of a Happy Life* and "You meaner beauties of the night." Of the poems in Milton's volume some had been printed before—the Latin *Naturam non pati senium* (probably), *On Shakespeare, Comus, Lycidas,* the second poem on Hobson, and *Epitaphium Damonis*(?). To these were now added nearly all the other early English poems, nearly all the Latin and Greek pieces of any account, the Italian sonnets, and five English sonnets.

We observed that in 1637, as Milton wrote to Diodati, he was working his way through the history of medieval Europe, and that entries in the Commonplace Book were predominantly from historians, ancient and modern, continental and English. During the years 1646–1648, a period in which he was not writing pamphlets, Milton made headway with a *History of Britain;* the first four books were completed by March, 1649. Because of official

duties, including the several *Defences*, he was not able
to take it up again until 1655, when he added two books
which carried the story to 1066. These six books were
published in 1670; in the years of the major poems Milton
evidently gave up hope of continuing the work.

As a critical student of sources, Milton was in the
new tradition of historiography—represented by William
Camden, Sir John Hayward, Samuel Daniel, and others—
which owed much to the classical historians and to such
moderns as Machiavelli. (Milton's own favorite was the
terse Sallust.) These English writers aimed at realistic
analyses of events and persons and policies, of causes
and effects. In regard to national beginnings, the new
rationalism did not cherish the mass of legend that for
centuries had led less sophisticated piety from Trojan
Brute through a long line of kings which included Lear
and Cymbeline. Milton, not without reluctance, made a
partial concession to the poetical—such as his own allusion in *Comus*,

> Virgin, daughter of Locrine,
> Sprung of old Anchises' line—

by rehearsing briefly some of the tales, but, like his
critical predecessors, he began history proper with Julius
Caesar's invasion. His anti-Romanist and anticlerical bias
contributed to his general skepticism about monkish
chronicles and to his slighting of ecclesiastical history.
Skepticism about King Arthur was presumably one reason for his abandonment of the Arthurian epic he had
conceived in 1638–1640; if, as scholars have remarked,
the *History* was in some sense a substitute, it was no
song of heroic triumph. Milton's aim was to compose a
true and coherent narrative. He held the full humanistic
belief in the didactic value of history, and his first page
indicates that he wrote with one eye on his own time.
His period and materials did not admit of much philo-

sophical interpretation, and he apparently did not share the active interest of his age in Saxon antiquities and institutions—an interest which led such diverse libertarians as Sir Edward Coke and John Lilburne and Gerrard Winstanley to see Saxon liberties crushed under "the Norman yoke." The new historiography had not precluded recognition of God's providence—a premise conspicuous in Shakespeare's historical plays and Ralegh's *History of the World*—and we might expect it to be strong in Milton. It appeared mainly in pessimistic form: the early conquests established his conviction—to be reiterated in the major poetical works—that when nations grow corrupt God lets them fall an easy prey to invaders; and the Britons and the Saxons were about equally guilty. The chief evidence of Milton's concern with his own time was the digression in Book 3 on the parallel between the confusion in Britain after the Romans left and that which in 1646–1648 followed the civil war. This section was deleted from the *History* of 1670, whether by the author or (according to Toland) by the censor, and was published separately in 1681. It might be called an expansion of the last lines of the sonnet to Fairfax (1648), a disillusioned outburst against self-seeking on the part of both laymen and clerics who were supposed to be forwarding the great reformation.

6

The Secretaryship and Political Tracts; Blindness

AFTER LONG AND DEVIOUS NEGOTIATIONS with the Scots, parliament, and the army, King Charles, taken over by the army, was tried by a court nominated by the "Rump" parliament (Presbyterians having been excluded by Colonel Pride's "Purge" of December 6, 1648), and was executed on January 30, 1649. Two weeks later appeared Milton's first political tract, *The Tenure of Kings and Magistrates*, his first publication in prose since 1645. When in the *Second Defence* (1654) he looked back upon the *Tenure*, he still heatedly remembered the Presbyterian ministers of London who had cried out against the sentence on the king as abhorrent to all Protestant doctrine (their real reason, he said, was not the sentence itself but the eclipsing of their party by the Independents). Milton had felt bound to attack so patent a falsehood and, avoiding the particular question of the king, he had (to translate his Latin)

only set forth in general terms, with many testimonies from the most authoritative divines, what may be lawfully done against tyrants. . . . This tract did not appear until after the king's death; it was intended rather to quiet men's minds than to render any decision about Charles, since that was the magistrates' business, not mine, and since the sentence had already been carried out.

From the Middle Ages onward, the central question
in political thought had been that of popular resistance
to civil or royal authority, and this, like all political questions, had its religious as well as secular complications.
Along with "Render unto Caesar the things that are
Caesar's," the biblical *locus classicus* was Romans 13:
"Let every soul be subject to the higher powers. . . ." But
Calvin, the pope of Protestantism, while he took the
orthodox position of nonresistance, allowed exceptions
in two kinds of cases: when resistance came from duly
constituted magistrates, and when secular commands
violated the individual conscience. Such exceptions left
the door ajar, and it was pushed open by subsequent
"democratic" thinkers, notably some Huguenots of the
later sixteenth century. In England the general problem
was exacerbated by the changing character and relations
of the crown and parliament and by the personal character and principles of King James and King Charles. The
Stuarts insisted on their divine right and their responsibility to none but God, in a way the chief Tudor sover-
eigns had been much too wise to do. On the other hand,
parliament, while respectful to the last toward the Lord's
Anointed, was increasingly determined to maintain what
it regarded as its ancient rights against the new absolutism. Political conflict was complicated and intensified
by the conflicts between Anglicans and Puritans and,
from about 1645 onward, by the splitting of the Puritans
into Presbyterian, Independent, and more or less anti-
nomian sects. Further, the army, in which Independency
was strong, had become a formidable political power,
though it also had its internal divisions, notably between
Cromwell and other "grandees" and the Levellers headed
by John Lilburne.

In his first pamphlet against the bishops Milton was,
we remember, a good monarchist who argued that the
throne was endangered by its episcopal allies. We do

not know by what steps he arrived at the position expounded in the *Tenure*, although, with the aid of his Commonplace Book, we might have guessed the direction his political thinking would take. The *Tenure* echoed political theorists from Aristotle up to 1649. If it presented no novel ideas, it was a reasoned and vigorous summary of traditional "democratic" thought in relation to the modern English setting, and, as we have observed, it was animated in no small degree by Milton's antipathy to recent Presbyterian "royalism." The gist of the argument is that the power of kings and magistrates

was and is originally the people's, and by them conferred in trust only to be employed to the common peace and benefit; with liberty therefore and right remaining in them to reassume it to themselves, if by kings or magistrates it be abused; or to dispose of it by any alteration, as they shall judge most conducing to the public good.

"Any alteration" includes the deposition or even execution of a tyrant, as indeed Milton's full title affirmed. Thus his view of that legal theorem, "the social contract," was the exact opposite of the view Hobbes was to set forth in *Leviathan* (1651), that the people surrender all their rights to the sovereign power, which may not be opposed. Milton's widow, by the way, told John Aubrey

that Mr. Hobbes was not one of his acquaintance, that her husband did not like him at all; but he would acknowledge him to be a man of great parts and a learned man. Their interests and tenets did run counter to each other—vide Mr. Hobbes' *Behemoth*.

In *Behemoth*, published some years after Milton's death, Hobbes linked together Salmasius' book and Milton's reply as examples of good Latin and ill reasoning.

In March, 1649, a month after the appearance of the *Tenure*, Milton, as an evident friend of the new régime and a scholar, was invited to become Secretary for Foreign Tongues to the Council of State. He was pressing on with his *History of Britain* and other studies, but, in addition to the claims of public service, he was doubtless attracted, as a writer hitherto on the sidelines, by the opportunity for direct participation. The post was not on the policy-making level. Milton's work was to write official letters, in Latin, to foreign governments and to digest foreign correspondence. Another part of his commission was to answer attacks made on the regicides and the Commonwealth by adherents of the royalist cause. On May 14, 1649, the young poet, essayist, and miscellaneous writer, John Hall, was appointed by the government to reply to such attacks, but Milton became the chief spokesman. We may skip his first official publication, *Articles of Peace* (May, 1649), which contained the Earl of Ormonde's treaty with the Irish rebels and other documents and Milton's "Observations" thereon.

He soon had to deal with something that was far more powerful than any direct attack and that may indeed be called the most immediately effective piece of propaganda ever issued in English. This was *Eikon Basilike: The Portraiture of His Sacred Majesty in his Solitudes and Sufferings* (February, 1649). The origins, materials, and authorship of this book have been debated for three centuries, but the authoritative modern view is that it was edited from the king's papers by his chaplain, the Reverend John Gauden, with the king's help and approval. A multitude of people, not merely royalists and Anglicans, had felt a shock of horror at the execution of a king and one who—as Marvell's famous lines record—had on the scaffold made a noble end. Such emotions were now crystallized and intensified by the stained-glass image of the royal martyr in captivity reviewing his actions in prayerful innocence—a figure whom some royalists could look back upon as "Christ the Second." Against such a wave of sentiment no recital of Charles's stubborn follies and duplicities could prevail at all, and Milton's *Eikonoklastes* (October, 1649) presumably changed no one's mind. He scored a debater's point in noting that one of the king's prayers had been taken from Sir Philip Sidney's *Arcadia*. In the *Second Defence* Milton felt able to say: "I did not, as is pretended, 'revile the dead sovereign'; I only wrote with the conviction that Queen Truth must be preferred to King Charles." But in 1660 the book was to be cited in the proclamation for Milton's arrest and publicly burned.

In 1649 Claudius Salmasius (Claude de Saumaise), perhaps the chief classical scholar in Europe, published *Defensio Regia pro Carolo I*, a work solicited by the exiled Charles II. Though it was at first anonymous, the authorship was well known, and Salmasius' name added large authority to his heavy-handed championship of divine right and his denunciation of the regicides. On January 8, 1650, Milton was instructed by the Council to compose an answer. In *Pro Populo Anglicano Defensio* (February, 1651)—written in Latin, since it was addressed to all Europe—Milton expanded the central doctrine of his *Tenure of Kings and Magistrates*. He appealed to God, right reason, and the law of nature, crushing Salmasius' biblical and historical examples under examples of popular sovereignty and exposing his ignorance of English institutions—all this peppered with allusions to a hired propagandist, a turncoat, a grammarian, a henpecked husband. "The great kill-cow of Christendom" (in Edward Phillips's phrase), who happened now to be sojourning at the court of Sweden, was effectively discredited, and no doubt the force of his charges against the Commonwealth suffered too. Nine years later, in his last effort to preserve the republic, Milton proudly recalled his victory over "a famous and thought invincible adversary."

Milton had been warned that continued labor would

probably extinguish what remained of his failing eyesight, but, as a crusader in a holy war, he persevered.
His eyes had been weak from boyhood and they began
to fail noticeably about 1644, according to a letter of
September 28, 1654, to the Greek Leonard Philaras, in
which Milton described his symptoms and their onset.
Expert modern diagnoses, necessarily based on this account by a seventeenth-century layman, have varied:
they include glaucoma, myopia, detachment of the retina,
and chiasmal pressure caused by a suprasellar cyst. The
sight of one eye was almost gone early in 1650 and blindness became complete in the winter of 1651–1652, when
Milton was only forty-three and the great poem was still
unwritten.

Milton was continued in his secretarial post, though
his work had to be lessened. One minor task, which he
performed from March, 1651, through January, 1652,
was the licensing of the newspaper *Mercurius Politicus*.
Its editor was the clever but unscrupulous Marchamont
Needham or Nedham, who had already changed sides
twice and was to change again. Some writers, eager to
find flaws in Milton, have seen a betrayal of *Areopagitica*
in his serving as "censor"; but he was apparently only
doing what is done by any editor-in-chief of a periodical
or any government official who supervises a departmental
publication. He could not remove the control ordered by
parliament, and the required job might have been done
worse by someone else.

In May, 1652, when Milton had had some months of
total blindness, his wife died, about three days after the
birth (May 2) of her daughter Deborah. The earlier
children were Anne (born July 29, 1646), Mary (October 25, 1648), and John (March 16, 1651), who died
soon after his mother.

In the first years of his blindness Milton spent much
labor, now more difficult labor, on his *Pro Populo*

Anglicano Defensio Secunda (May, 1654), a reply to an anonymous attack of 1652 on the Commonwealth regicides, *Regii Sanguinis Clamor ad Coelum* (*The Cry of the Royal Blood to Heaven*); this book included scurrilous falsehoods about Milton. It had been written by a cleric, Peter du Moulin, but was seen through the press by another cleric, Alexander More, who wrote a preface over the printer's signature. In accordance with common talk and belief and the reports of Secretary Thurloe's agents, Milton treated More as the author, and drubbed him unmercifully for scandalous behavior, in particular the seducing of Salmasius' wife's maid. Just before his book was published, Milton was told that More was not the author, but this information had started from More himself and no one revealed the true author's name; in such circumstances Milton went ahead. Apart from the unsavory personal material, the *Second Defence* was a much finer work than the reply to Salmasius. Milton's outline of his own career, evoked by Du Moulin's charges of misconduct, has been repeatedly cited in earlier pages. The passage on his blindness—an affliction, enemies said, that was a divine judgment—is a partial parallel to the invocation to Light in *Paradise Lost*. In both Milton's feeling is dramatized and sublimated in an impersonal way: as a spokesman for truth, he links himself with the blind seers of antiquity, and—as Socrates could propose, instead of the death penalty, support at the public expense—so Milton can claim to be "not only safe from men's injuries but, as it were, sacred and immune."

His hopes for the revolution, which had been so depressed by parliamentary and Presbyterian shortcomings and corruption, have been revived by Cromwell's leadership, and he feels again the high heroic mood of earlier years. He rejoices in what the Commonwealth has so far accomplished and looks forward to still greater things. At the same time, even in eulogizing the Protector, who has proved his right to govern by his ability to govern himself, Milton warns of the dangers of a dictatorship and urges Cromwell to remember the services and capacities of his associates. As a resolute champion of individual freedom of conscience, he opposes what Cromwell had come to favor, a state church (though Cromwell's idea was broadly comprehensive and tolerant). Milton would have a state-supported system of education. And, since the multiplication of laws is undesirable and ineffectual, he maintains that liberty—which includes liberty of the press—is the best school of virtue.

The long *Pro Se Defensio* (August, 1655), a reply to More's reply to the *Second Defence*, was a mopping-up operation, conducted with much tactical skill and with the energy of a man who identified defense of himself with defense of his country. His acknowledgment of a mistake about the authorship of the *Clamor* would make less impression on readers than the elaborated charges—which recent research has verified—against More's character and career.

As we have just seen, Milton was engaged during 1649–1655 in answering enemies of the Commonwealth, and that work along with his blindness had necessitated relief from some of his ordinary secretarial functions, although up through 1659 he was still translating state papers. In 1653 he strongly recommended Andrew Marvell as an assistant; though Marvell was not appointed until 1657, from 1653 onward Milton was only one of the secretaries under John Thurloe. In April, 1655, his salary, which had been £288, was ordered reduced to £150 as a pension for life, but in 1659 he was receiving a salary of £200.

7

Sonnets

SINCE MILTON'S LATER PAMPHLETS on national questions belong to 1659–1660, we may postpone them and look at the seventeen sonnets of 1642–1658. These fall into two groups, public and private (though a few are both), which differ widely in style as in theme; all of course are far from the amatory sequences of the Elizabethans. As we should expect of such a lover of Italian literature, Milton used the Petrarchan form, not the English pattern of three quatrains and a couplet. For the sonnets on heroic themes he had the special precedent of Tasso, and, in spirit though not in form, the patriotic odes of Horace. As Wordsworth said,

> when a damp
> Fell round the path of Milton, in his hand
> The Thing became a trumpet; whence he blew
> Soul-animating strains—alas, too few!

Of the three recent sonnets included in the *Poems* of 1645 the first, "Captain or colonel, or knight in arms"— the word "colonel" has three syllables—was in the heroic vein. It was written toward the middle of November, 1642, not quite three months after the outbreak of war, when the royalist army, after the battle of Edgehill, had advanced to the outskirts of London. The Cambridge

Manuscript gives two titles, the first deleted (Milton printed neither), "On his door when the city expected an assault" and "When the assault was intended to the city." We need not imagine that Milton pinned the sonnet on his door or had any thought of doing so; he was only using a dramatic device for an impersonal utterance. The octave presents the humanist-poet whose art creates the fame of men of action; the sestet recalls two anecdotes from Greek history, Alexander's sparing Pindar's house when he razed the city of Thebes and the Spartans' refraining from the destruction of Athens when one of their officers recited the first chorus of Euripides' *Electra*. Here, as in the later heroic sonnets, we have the beginnings of the grand style and hints of its functional value: for instance, the periphrasis, "The great Emathian conqueror," is not mere inflation; it heightens the idea of power in contrast with the humble "house of Pindarus."

Under public sonnets may be included two satirical pieces, presumably of 1645–1646, expressing Milton's reaction to the attacks upon his pamphlets on divorce. One, "A book was writ of late called *Tetrachordon*," in a colloquial style with rhymes that anticipate Byron and Browning, carries a half-humorous contempt for an age that is puzzled by a Greek title but can stomach the Scottish names made familiar by Scottish participation in the civil war. The second of the pair (actually written first), "I did but prompt the age to quit their clogs," combines journalism and simple sublimity, disillusionment with God's Englishmen and the affirmation of a central Miltonic principle. To 1646 perhaps belongs the "tailed" sonnet, *On the New Forcers of Conscience under the Long Parliament*. Here, as in *Areopagitica*, Milton assails the English and Scottish Presbyterians—some of them by name—who have set up their own tyranny in place of the episcopal, and he ends with the famous line, soundly etymological and satirical, "New Presbyter is but

old Priest writ large." Even in this rough tirade, as in
other sonnets, or, for that matter, his first Elegy with its
allusion to Ovid's exile, Milton links his cause and the
men he admires with the great of the past:

> Men whose life, learning, faith and pure intent
>   Would have been held in high esteem with Paul
>   Must now be named and printed heretics
> By shallow Edwards and Scotch what-d'ye-call.

To digress briefly from the sonnets, on January 23,
1647, Milton addressed a Latin poem to John Rous,
keeper of the Bodleian Library, to whom he had sent a
copy of his *Poems*, with the eleven pamphlets he had so
far published. The *Poems* had been lost in transit and
in replacing the gift Milton added this poem, his last of
any account in Latin, an irregular ode in a pattern somewhat akin to the Pindaric. The Ode—like the sonnet
"Captain or colonel"—might be called "Reflections in wartime on the value of poetry." Whatever his public and
private disappointments, Milton displays an urbane and
even playful idealism at once detached and dedicated,
and sees poetry and culture and the Bodleian outliving
the tumult of war. In April, 1648, when the Westminster Assembly was actively concerned about a new
psalter, Milton the classicist gave way to the Hebraist:
he made metrical translations of a group of Psalms
(80–88) in the common style (and with echoes of earlier
versions), though he took pains to indicate the phrases
he added to the Hebrew. In August, 1653, he translated
another group (1–8) in various meters. It is a question
how far literary and public motives were mixed with
religious and private consolation in both groups, especially the second.

The year 1648 brought royalist uprisings, the so-called
second civil war, and the Scottish invasion, and in
the summer Sir Thomas Fairfax's siege of Colchester

prompted a sonnet in praise of the parliamentary general, who in 1645 had won the decisive battle of Naseby. The octave celebrated Fairfax's military prowess. The sestet was at once an exhortation to him and another testimony to Milton's loss of faith in the Long Parliament:

> O yet a nobler task awaits thy hand;
>> For what can war but endless war still breed,
>> Till truth and right from violence be freed,
> And public faith cleared from the shameful brand
>> Of public fraud? In vain doth valor bleed
>> While avarice and rapine share the land.

But Fairfax recoiled from the execution of the king and the invasion of Scotland and in 1650 withdrew from public life to the pastoral peace of Nun Appleton in Yorkshire (where Marvell, his daughter's tutor, wrote the poetry by which he lives); and Milton, renewing his praises in the *Second Defence*, saw him as another Scipio in retirement.

In the month of his first wife's death Milton addressed a sonnet—to quote the manuscript title—*To the Lord General Cromwell, May 1652, on the proposals of certain ministers at the Committee for Propagation of the Gospel.* Like Fairfax, Cromwell is glorified for his military victories but summoned to the works of peace. The particular occasion is that

> new foes arise
> Threat'ning to bind our souls with secular chains.
>> Help us to save free conscience from the paw
>> Of hireling wolves whose gospel is their maw.

The "wolves" are not now the Roman Catholics of *Lycidas* but those ministers—some of them Independents who had stood out against the Westminster Assembly—who want to license and thus control the irregular preachers so numerous in these unsettled times, a form of religious censorship abhorrent to Milton.

In July of this year Milton wrote a sonnet to Sir Henry Vane, who, since war with Holland had lately begun, was head of a committee treating with the Dutch ambassadors. But the poem rises above immediate circumstances. As governor of Massachusetts in 1636–1637, when in his twenties, Sir Henry had courageously defended Anne Hutchinson against repressive religious authorities, and in the Westminster Assembly he had argued for freedom of conscience. Milton links him as a statesman with senators of the Roman republic and praises his understanding of the different functions of the spiritual and the civil sword. In his religious individualism Milton was closer to Vane than to Cromwell, who, as we observed, upheld a comprehensive established church.

The last and greatest of Milton's heroic sonnets was that tremendous prayer and invective, "Avenge, O Lord, thy slaughtered saints," on the massacre, in April, 1655, of the Piedmontese Protestants by Italian troops. In his role as secretary, Milton drafted letters of protest sent by Cromwell to the Duke of Savoy and France and several Protestant countries. The sonnet is a capital example of the way in which Milton's sonnets tend to resemble massive paragraphs of blank verse. The octave ends and the sestet begins in the middle of line 10. The rhyme words are notably sonorous—"bones," "cold," "old," "stones," "groans," and the like—yet the combination of run-on lines and pronounced medial pauses and stops almost obliterates the formal pattern. These and other freedoms, such as the wrenching of natural word order, Milton may have learned especially from Giovanni della Casa, though he far surpassed his model in power.

Of the private sonnets, two were written early enough to be included in the *Poems* of 1645. Of these two the better one was addressed to Lady Margaret Ley, whom Milton, after his wife left him, "made it his chief diversion now and then in an evening to visit." She, says

Phillips, "being a woman of great wit and ingenuity, had a particular honor for him and took much delight in his company, as likewise her husband, Captain Hobson, a very accomplished gentleman." This sonnet combines a heroic octave, in praise of Lady Margaret's father, the Earl of Marlborough, with a sestet in praise of her. The father had held high offices under James and Charles and had died in 1629, a few days after the dissolution of the last parliament to be called until 1640. Despite his royalist affiliation, he is honored as an exemplar of old-fashioned integrity, and, in Milton's way, he is given large stature by being linked with Isocrates, "that old man eloquent," who was said to have starved himself to death after the battle of Chaeronea "fatal to liberty."

In a sonnet dated February 9, 1646, "To my friend, Mr. Henry Lawes," and printed as a commendatory piece in Lawes's *Choice Psalms* (1648), Milton paid high tribute to his old musical associate, who had been named on the title page of his own *Poems* as composer of music for the songs. As a court musician, Lawes was naturally a royalist. Like Lady Margaret's father and other men, he is endowed with more than modern dignity through an illustrious comparison—with the musician Casella whom Dante "Met in the milder shades of Purgatory." A sonnet of serene piety and biblical imagery honored "the religious memory" of Mrs. Thomason, who died in December, 1646; her husband, George Thomason, is held in something like religious memory by all modern students of the period for his having collected and dated over 22,000 books and pamphlets published during 1640–1661.

The date of Milton's best-known sonnet, "When I consider how my light is spent," has been much disputed. Its position in the *Poems* of 1673 might seem to place it in 1655, but that argument fails when it is shown that the order of the sonnets, while roughly chronological, is not strictly so. And, regardless of bibliography, most readers must feel certain that the sonnet expresses Milton's first reaction to the shock of complete blindness; it would therefore have been composed early in 1652 or possibly at the end of 1651, not long after he reached forty-three. The sonnet takes us back to "How soon hath Time," written probably on his twenty-fourth birthday. The parable of the talents now weighs much more heavily upon him, and his desire to serve his Maker has the full force of much-tried maturity and apparent frustration; but, under a blow so calamitous for a scholar and writer, he rallies all his faith to accept God's ways and appointed service.

If Horace's exalted appeals to the old Roman virtues contributed to Milton's heroic sonnets, Horace's lower note of genial hospitality helped to set the tone of invitations to two young friends. Both were composed in or about 1655. One was addressed to Edward Lawrence, the son of a prominent member of the Cromwellian government, who was offered a neat repast "Of Attic taste, with wine," and the lute or Italian song; presumably these amenities were available in Milton's house, and they also suggested traditional symposia. The other sonnet carried a less epicurean but also Horatian invitation to Milton's former pupil, Cyriack Skinner, grandson of Sir Edward Coke and himself a lawyer. It is good to know of Milton's readiness, in his later and darker years, to "waste a sullen day" by the fire and drench deep thoughts in mirth. These relaxed sonnets have both charm and dignity, and they remind us of Milton's capacity for making and keeping young friends as well as old ones.

A second sonnet to Skinner, on the third anniversary of his blindness—"Cyriack, this three years' day" (1655)—shows not merely the religious submission and trust of 1652 but heroic fortitude and confidence. Though Milton's sight is bereft

> Of sun or moon or star throughout the year,
> Or man or woman—

a catalogue shorter and even simpler than that in the invocation to Light—

> Yet I argue not
> Against Heav'n's hand or will, nor bate a jot
> Of heart or hope, but still bear up and steer
> Right onward.

He has the consciousness of having lost his sight in defending liberty before all Europe, and a stronger support than that:

> This thought might lead me through the world's
> vain masque,
> Content though blind, had I no better guide.

Milton's last sonnet, and one of his two or three finest ones, was "Methought I saw my late espoused saint," the passionate, tender, and reverent vision of the wife whom he had recently married and lost. On November 12, 1656, he had married Katherine Woodcock, who gave birth to a child in October, 1657, and died in February, 1658, when she was not quite thirty; the child died a few weeks later. The octave is a grandly simple example of Milton's instinctive use of both classical and Hebraic traditions—the allusion to Alcestis brought back from the grave and the purification of women after childbirth "in the old Law." In his dream he cannot describe his wife's face, since he had probably never seen her. She

> Came vested all in white, pure as her mind.
> Her face was veiled, yet to my fancied sight
> Love, sweetness, goodness in her person shined
> So clear as in no face with more delight.
> But O as to embrace me she inclined,
> I waked, she fled, and day brought back my night.

The last line is an instance of pregnant and poignant
"wit." We may think of this sonnet when we encounter
echoes of Dr. Johnson's charge about Milton's "Turkish
contempt of females"; we may think too of the contrast
between Milton's outgoing devotion and Donne's self-
centered sonnet on his wife's death.

8

Tracts of 1659–1660

WE NOW TURN BACK to public affairs and prose. On September 3, 1658, the anniversary of his victories at Dunbar and Worcester, Cromwell died. In the funeral procession on November 23 walked a group of "Secretaries of the French and Latin Tongues," Milton, Marvell, Samuel Hartlib, Nathaniel Sterry, and apparently the young John Dryden (who was twitted after 1660 with having been a clerk under Cromwell). The Protector was succeeded, in dynastic fashion, by his son Richard. But Richard was quite unable to cope with the warring leaders and factions who had sorely tried his masterful father, and the twenty months between Oliver's death and Charles's return were a period of general confusion.

Since 1653, as we saw, Milton had been only one of the secretaries and his duties had been curtailed, so that, after *Pro Se Defensio* (1655) was off his hands, he had more free time. During 1655–1660 he worked on the *History of Britain* and the large Latin treatise, *De Doctrina Christiana*, and presumably composed a good deal of *Paradise Lost*. In the spring of 1658 he edited, from a manuscript in his possession, *The Cabinet Council*, a political treatise which, until recently, was attributed to Sir Walter Ralegh. But Milton had not withdrawn his attention from public affairs and he had not quite lost the Puritan vision of the holy community. In 1659 he addressed two tracts to parliament. The first was *A Treatise of Civil Power in Ecclesiastical Causes: showing that it is not lawful for any power on earth to compel in matters of religion* (February). This was a statement, "drawn from the scripture only," of Milton's prime doctrine of "Christian liberty," the inalienable right of the individual Christian to be guided by his understanding of the Bible and the illumination of the Holy Spirit, without any interference from civil or ecclesiastical authority. He had moved from Independency to independence. In other areas than the religious the doctrine had revolutionary, even anarchic, potentialities: the individual Christian owes no necessary allegiance to any external institution. The second tract of 1659 likewise recalls the Puritan and Miltonic concern with the ideal of the apostolic church and Milton's special antipathy to any kind of establishment. The title will be enough: *Considerations Touching the Likeliest Means to Remove Hirelings out of the Church: wherein is also discoursed of Tithes, Church Fees, Church Revenues, and whether any maintenance of ministers can be settled by law* (August). One special point, which arises in regard to ministers' having a gainful secular occupation, is Milton's demand for free universal education and vocational training. Neither pamphlet seems to have attracted attention.

But the next one brought royalist gibes and renewed and hazardous notoriety for its author. In February or the first days of March, 1660, appeared *The Ready and Easy Way to Establish a Free Commonwealth, and the Excellence Thereof Compared with the Inconveniences and Dangers of Readmitting Kingship in this Nation.* This tract—which had a revised and much enlarged edition in April—and a letter to General Monck (late March) and a reply to a royalist sermon (April) were pleas from the staunch republican on the eve of the Restoration, and they testify to his courage, not to say recklessness. On February 3 General Monck, with the troops he had led down from Scotland, had entered London and proceeded to take charge of chaotic affairs. He quickly summoned the Long Parliament, including the members who had been shut out by Pride's Purge of December, 1648; this body, after issuing writs for a new election, dissolved on March 16. But the readmission of excluded members on February 21 had made pretty clear the course of things to come. And over a much longer time a large share of public sentiment had been turning toward the Restoration: there was nostalgia, heightened by Puritan strictness concerning manners and morals and by recent disorder and economic depression, for "the good old times"; and a desire for the return not only of the monarchy but of a real parliament and of the Church of England. One factor that helped to translate sentiment into action was the alliance between Anglican royalists and what Milton calls "new royalized Presbyterians."

Milton outlined a republican constitution which would vest central authority in a grand council; the historical scholar appealed to ancient precedents in Judea, Athens, and republican Rome, and to modern ones in the States-General of the United Provinces of the Netherlands and the council of Venice (the special ideal of seventeenth-century republicans). This grand council, renewed if necessary by partial rotation (a reluctant concession to the much-discussed ideas of James Harrington), would be perpetual. There would be a smaller executive council; and county assemblies would have charge of local affairs and would also pass judgment on the grand council's legislation. Such a constitution, Milton told his readers, would preserve and enlarge the internal reforms and national prestige achieved by the Commonwealth, and would ensure wise and frugal government, civil and religious liberty, popular education, a responsible body of citizens, prosperity and general content. But the mass of people had no more interest in Milton's "unrealistic" plan than in his wholly accurate prophecy of the consequences of restored kingship.

In his leftward evolution since 1641, and in his writings of the early months of 1660, Milton's theoretical and practical thinking necessarily responded in some degree to the changing posture of events, parties, and powers. There was a gap between the ideal and the doubtfully possible. To sum up his later position, in comparison with that of other radical individuals and groups, he was not a democrat in the full modern sense. He was rather a classical or "aristocratic" republican, a believer in the rule of the best, not of the many; throughout his writings Athens and Rome appear as the nurseries of true liberty. While Milton had read many historians and political thinkers, old and new, one main part of his ideal was the Platonic philosopher-king. But this conception was fused with one no less "aristocratic" in the religious sense, the Puritan ideal of the rule of the saints, who, like the biblical Israelites, were an island of righteousness in the sea of the world; by 1660, however, the number of these seemed to have shrunk almost to the vanishing point. The humanist and the Puritan coalesce in one central and unchanging principle, continually reiterated in Milton's prose and verse and notably in the epics and *Samson*, that the maintenance of outward liberty depends on the inward liberty, responsibility, and integrity of individual citizens.

It may be observed that in the tracts of 1659–1660—in keeping with the general development of prose and with Milton's deepening concentration on religion and the individual conscience—his style is relatively disciplined, plain, lucid, and unfigurative. Two passages to be quoted in a moment are exceptional outbursts of prophetic fervor. Indeed the great importance of the *Ready and*

Easy Way for the understanding of Milton and the poems still to come is less political than emotional. In spite of the proposals he makes, he has almost no hope of overcoming "this noxious humor of returning to bondage." We remember the triumphant prayer that concluded *Of Reformation in England*, the surging confidence of *Areopagitica*—"Methinks I see in my mind a noble and puissant nation . . ."—and now we read this:

That a nation should be so valorous and courageous to win their liberty in the field, and when they have won it, should be so heartless and unwise in their counsels as not to know how to use it, value it, what to do with it or with themselves, but after ten or twelve years' prosperous war and contestation with tyranny, basely and besottedly to run their necks again into the yoke which they have broken, and prostrate all the fruits of their victory for naught at the feet of the vanquished, besides our loss of glory, and such an example as kings or tyrants never yet had the like to boast of, will be an ignominy, if it befall us, that never yet befell any nation possessed of their liberty, worthy indeed themselves, whatsoever they be, to be for ever slaves. . . .

The most bitter eloquence of all is the final paragraph, a last cry of despair over the ruin of all the hopes to which Milton had given nearly twenty years of arduous labor and his eyesight:

What I have spoken is the language of that which is not called amiss "The good old Cause"; if it seem strange to any, it will not seem more strange, I hope, than convincing to backsliders. Thus much I should perhaps have said, though I were sure I should have spoken only to trees and stones; and had none to cry to but with the prophet, "O earth, earth, earth!" to tell the very soil itself what her perverse inhabitants are deaf to. Nay, though what I have spoke should happen (which Thou suffer not, who didst create mankind free! nor Thou next, who didst redeem us from being servants of men!) to be the last words of our expiring liberty. But I trust I shall

have spoken persuasion to abundance of sensible and ingenu-
ous men; to some, perhaps, whom God may raise of these
stones to become children of reviving liberty; and may re-
claim, though they seem now choosing them a captain back
for Egypt, to bethink themselves a little and consider whither
they are rushing; to exhort this torrent also of the people not
to be so impetuous, but to keep their due channel; and at
length recovering and uniting their better resolutions, now
that they see already how open and unbounded the insolence
and rage is of our common enemies, to stay these ruinous
proceedings, justly and timely fearing to what a precipice of
destruction the deluge of this epidemic madness would hurry
us, through the general defection of a misguided and abused
multitude.

In April, as we saw, Milton published an enlarged
version of this tract, and on May 29 Charles II made his
triumphal entry into London. He was quickly hailed by
Dryden, Waller, and Cowley—but not by Marvell—with
eulogies which they hoped might obliterate their eulogies
(in Cowley's case a veiled one) of Cromwell. Charles
was not "the eternal and shortly expected King" whom
Milton had ecstatically envisioned in 1641, whose return
he had in 1649 prayed might be soon and in 1660 could
still appeal to as a certain but apparently remote event.

PART FOUR

The Restoration

1660–1674

Personal Danger and Settled Life

THE PASSAGES just quoted from the *Ready and Easy Way* are enough to suggest what the Restoration meant for Milton. It would strain to the utmost even his faith in God's providence to accept the nation's return to bondage. Whatever relative peace, outward and inward, time was to bring, the composition of the three major works of Milton's later years would renew his sense of heroic past and ignoble present and would reflect the shift of his concern from public and militant action to the fortitude of the individual soul.

But there were more immediately personal troubles to face. In 1660 a dozen regicides were executed (and Sir Henry Vane in 1662); two dozen men were imprisoned for life; and some twenty escaped from the country. On January 30, 1661, the twelfth anniversary of Charles I's execution, the exhumed bodies of Cromwell, Henry Ireton, and John Bradshaw were hanged at Tyburn and their heads were set on poles at Westminster Hall. Milton, as the great defender of the regicides and the Commonwealth, a man who up to the last moment had vehemently opposed the Restoration, was in very real danger of death or imprisonment. In May or early June, 1660, his friends took him into hiding in Bartholomew Close, Smithfield. On June 16 the House of Commons passed a resolution for the impounding and burning of his first *Defensio* and *Eikonoklastes* and a tract by the Reverend John Goodwin and the arrest of both men; the public proclamation to this effect, however, was not made until August 13 and then concerned only the books, the authors not having been found for trial. On June 18, in a House debate on the last of twenty men to be excepted from a general pardon, Milton's name was proposed by one speaker but not seconded. In the Act of Pardon, which became law on August 29, Milton was not named among the excepted, so that he was now virtually safe from serious danger. According to Edward Phillips, Milton's chief protector was Andrew Marvell; according to Jonathan Richardson, it was Sir William Davenant, the royalist playwright and poet. Marvell's active aid seems certain; possibly Davenant, though he lacked influence, had a share (Milton was said to have befriended Davenant, perhaps in the procuring of his pardon in 1654). Marvell and more prominent parliamentary friends, such as Arthur Annesley (later Earl of Anglesey), may have persuaded the authorities that Milton was now blind, harmless, and only a writer. Some of the meager and mystifying data suggest an understanding between friends and officials that the public calling in and burning of his books would serve to gloss over his being included in the general pardon. But, perhaps because the Sergeant-at-Arms was kept in the dark, Milton was actually arrested, we do not know just when (on September 12 he was not listed among prisoners then in the Sergeant's custody); he had to sue for pardon, which he may have done with reluctance and some delay. On December 15 the House ordered his pardon and release. A complaint was promptly made by Marvell against excessive fees—£150— charged by the Sergeant-at-Arms, fees which, however excessive, suggest more than brief confinement; indeed the record of Milton's release (December 17) speaks of his "having now laid long in custody."

To jump up for a moment to 1663 or later, the Restoration government, if we are to believe several witnesses, made overtures to its old enemy. The anonymous biographer says that Milton "was visited at his house on Bunhill by a chief officer of state, and desired to employ his pen on their behalf." If that meant defending the government, it would seem quite incredible; Milton was no Needham. A less implausible version was given by Richardson, "that . . . the King offered to employ this pardoned man as his Latin Secretary, the post in which he served Cromwell with so much integrity and ability," and that, when his wife urged acceptance, Milton said, "You, as other women, would ride in your coach; for me, my aim is to live and die an honest man." Milton's former chief, John Thurloe, was invited back (and declined); Marvell in 1659 had begun a parliamentary career of notable probity.

While by the end of 1660 Milton was free from the danger of official reprisals (although Richardson tells, whether reliably or not, of his having a continued fear of assassination), some other private troubles went on. His paternal inheritance and his secretarial salary (1649–1654, £288; 1655–1659, £200) had given him for a dozen years a comfortable income. But Commonwealth taxes and personal losses had been heavy. "Out of his secretary's salary," according to the anonymous biographer, "he had saved two thousand pounds, which, being lodged in the excise, and that bank failing upon the Restoration, he utterly lost." Phillips tells the same story and adds the loss of "another great sum, by mismanagement and for want of good advice" (the cause reported by a granddaughter was a scrivener's dishonesty). In the Great Fire of 1666 Milton lost the old family house in Bread Street, the sole property he owned apart from his residence near Bunhill Fields. At his death his estate was less than £1000, and the fact implies economy in previous years. Two testimonies help to fill out the picture. The anonymous biographer says that

constant frugality . . . enabled him at first to live within compass of the moderate patrimony his father left him, and afterwards to bear with patience, and no discomposure of his way of living, the great losses which befell him in his fortunes. Yet he was not sparing to buy good books, of which he left a fair collection; and was generous in relieving the wants of his friends.

John Toland related that

Towards the latter part of his time he contracted his library, both because the heirs he left could not make a right use of it, and that he thought he might sell it more to their advantage than they could be able to do themselves. His enemies reported that poverty constrained him thus to part with his books.

Blindness Milton had in some sense grown accustomed to, although we must never forget the immeasurable burden and handicap the scholar and poet endured. Besides the two great supports appealed to in his second sonnet to Cyriack Skinner, he got some small comfort from not being disfigured. Another prolonged and severe affliction, not in this case the traditional result of high living, was gout, "insomuch that his knuckles were all callous, yet was he not ever observed to be very impatient." One caller, a Dorsetshire clergyman, told Richardson that he

found John Milton, sitting in an elbow chair, black clothes and neat enough, pale but not cadaverous, his hands and fingers gouty and with chalk stones. Among other discourse he expressed himself to this purpose: that was he free from the pain this gave him, his blindness would be tolerable.

This report of the advanced state of the disease, and Milton's saying nothing of it in his extant letters, suggest to a recent medical investigator that a first and isolated attack may have occurred about 1665. During his last four years Milton would have had increasing and almost continuous pain and would have walked with difficulty. He evidently avoided the common and ineffectual remedies and his temperate regimen and exercises with a pulley were as good as anything he could do.

Aubrey and others give us details about the normal routine of Milton's later life. He got up at four o'clock and at four-thirty a man read to him from the Hebrew Bible.

Then he contemplated. At 7 his man came to him again, and then read to him, and wrote till dinner; the writing was as much as the reading. . . . After dinner he used to walk 3 or 4 hours at a time (he always had a garden where he lived); went to bed about 9.

At bedtime he had, like the ascetic poet-priest of his early sixth Elegy, a glass of water, and one is glad to hear of a solace that poem had not celebrated, a pipe. Evenings, the anonymous biographer relates, Milton

spent in reading some choice poets, by way of refreshment after the day's toil, and to store his fancy against morning. Besides his ordinary lectures out of the Bible and the best commentators on the week day, that was his sole subject on Sundays. And David's Psalms were in esteem with him above all poetry.

Toland, the skeptical deist, reports that

in the latter part of his life he was not a professed member of any particular sect among Christians, he frequented none of their assemblies, nor made use of their peculiar rites in his family.

Dr. Johnson, the devout Anglican, while regretting Milton's neglect of "any visible worship," public or domestic, added, with fine candor: "That he lived without prayer can hardly be affirmed; his studies and meditations were an habitual prayer."

In addition to paid assistants, and two daughters, there were, says Phillips, adults "who of their own accord greedily catched at the opportunity of being his readers," for their profit and his benefit; and "others of younger years" were "sent by their parents to the same end." Among volunteers were former pupils and such later friends as Thomas Ellwood, a young Quaker, whom Milton helped with his Latin. Milton needed both readers and writers, and the latter, like the former, might be regular employees, or on occasion a visiting nephew or friend might serve; the payment of outsiders must have been an item in the domestic economy during 1660–1674. (Aubrey mentions Deborah as an amanuensis, though in 1660 she was only eight.) As invocations in *Paradise Lost* remind us, Milton was much given to composing at night, and if the amanuensis came later than usual in the morning, "he would complain, saying *he wanted to be milked.*" A common posture for dictation was "leaning backward obliquely in an easy chair, with his leg flung over the elbow of it." Phillips says that he read *Paradise Lost*

from the very beginning, for some years, as I went from time to time to visit him, in a parcel of ten, twenty, or thirty verses at a time, which, being written by whatever hand came next, might possibly want correction as to the orthography and pointing.

And, Phillips goes on, when he asked why the stream dried up in the summer, his uncle replied "that his vein never happily flowed but from the autumnal equinoctial to the vernal, and that whatever he attempted [at other times] was never to his satisfaction, though he courted his fancy never so much. . . ." References in Milton's verse and prose, early and late, attest his sensitivity to climatic influence.

Music remained a continual resource, as the biographers relate. "He had," says Aubrey, "a delicate tuneable voice and had good skill. . . . He had an organ in his house; he played on that most. . . . Of a very cheerful humor. . . . He would be cheerful even in his gout fits and sing."

One feature of Milton's later life was both a pleasure and a trial, the number of callers, English and foreign, who wanted to see the renowned conqueror of Salmasius, the great relic of an age gone by. (In time, some came to see the author of *Paradise Lost*.) Speaking of his residence in Westminster (1652–1660), Phillips says what was more or less true of his last twenty years, that Milton

was frequently visited by persons of quality, particularly my Lady Ranelagh, whose son for some time he instructed; all learned foreigners of note, who could not part out of this city without giving a visit to a person so eminent. . . .

Phillips named some English friends and admirers, Marvell, Edward Lawrence (to whom Milton addressed a sonnet), Marchamont Needham, and especially Cyriack Skinner. For a time in the early 1650's Roger Williams exchanged lessons in Dutch for Milton's help with other languages. A "great admirer" of the later period was Sir Robert Howard the dramatist. Richardson had been told that Milton

used to sit in a grey coarse cloth coat at the door of his house, near Bunhill Fields without Moorgate, in warm sunny weather to enjoy the fresh air and so, as well as in his room, received the visits of people of distinguished parts as well as quality.

The Earl of Anglesey, who had been an important M.P. and probable champion in Milton's time of danger in 1660,

came often here to visit him, as very much coveting his society and converse; as likewise others of the nobility, and many persons of eminent quality; nor were the visits of foreigners ever more frequent than in this place, almost to his dying day.

According to Aubrey,

He was mightily importuned to go into France and Italy. Foreigners came much to see him and much admired him, and offered to him great preferments to come over to them: and the only inducement of several foreigners that came over into England was chiefly to see Oliver Protector and Mr. John Milton; and would see the house and chamber where he was born. He was much more admired abroad than at home.

Thus what Milton in his last Cambridge prolusion had depicted as a glorious reward of study had in some degree come true:

To be the oracle of many peoples; to have a house like a temple; to be [one of] those whom kings and nations invite to join them; one whom neighbors and strangers flock together to see, and a single glimpse of whom is taken by some as an achievement to boast about.

In conversation Milton is said to have been dignified, cheerful, lively, and often satirical. Aubrey, always alert for the vivid detail, records that "He pronounced the letter R (littera canina) very hard. ('A certain sign of a satirical wit'—from John Dryden)."

On February 24, 1663, Milton took a third wife, one Elizabeth Minshull, aged twenty-four, who had been "recommended to him by his old friend Dr. Paget"; she was a relative of Paget's. Elizabeth Milton seems to have been an affectionate wife and helpmate; Aubrey's phrase was "a gentle person, a peaceful and agreeable humor." She may not have been too gentle to put an end to the cheating of Milton by servants, and she was intellectual and loyal enough to preserve letters sent to him by scholars at home and abroad. We may welcome her declaration that "the pictures before his books are not *at all* like him"—though doubtless an exception should be made of the Faithorne portrait of 1670.

At the time of his third marriage Milton's oldest daughter, the crippled Anne, was sixteen, Mary fourteen, and Deborah eleven. Their mother had died in May, 1652, and they had had a stepmother only from the end of 1656 to the beginning of 1658. Their and their blind father's ordinary difficulties can be readily imagined, and a special one is notorious. Phillips said that two daughters (the eldest being excused perhaps because of infirmity of body and speech) were "condemned" to "a trial of patience almost beyond endurance," the reading aloud from books in languages they could pronounce but did not at all understand—Hebrew ("and I think the Syriac"), Greek, Latin, Italian, Spanish, and French. Phillips' list of languages must be exaggerated; Aubrey names Latin, Italian, French, and Greek. When this irksome employment led to some kind of rebellion (what Phillips calls "expressions of uneasiness"), the daughters "were all (even the eldest also) sent out to learn some curious and ingenious sorts of manufacture, that are proper for women to learn, particularly embroideries in gold or silver." This arrangement, made apparently in 1669–1670, may have been Mrs. Milton's. It must, at considerable expense, have eased the situation on both sides; we do not know what had been the actual extent of either painful services or consequent friction and may forbear comment on either filial or paternal shortcomings. At any rate our impressions are somewhat modified by Richardson's report of Deborah's later feelings. To many inquirers she

spoke of him with great tenderness: particularly I have been told she said he was delightful company, the life of the conversation, and that on account of a flow of subject and an unaffected cheerfulness and civility.

Richardson tells of her brushing aside some supposed portraits of Milton and fixing on a lifelike one, exclaim-

ing, "in a transport: ' 'Tis my father, 'tis my dear father!
I see him! 'Tis him!' "*

Apart from Milton's marriage and the publication of
books, the chief event of his quiet later life was his being
driven by the Great Plague to the village of Chalfont
St. Giles in Buckinghamshire. Not only were deaths
rapidly multiplying in London but the Bunhill district
had been chosen for one of the "pest-fields" or pits for
wholesale burial. The rural refuge, which had been found
at Milton's request by his young Quaker friend, Thomas
Ellwood, who lived in the neighborhood, was the home
of the poet and his family perhaps from June, 1665, until
February, 1666. The small house has been preserved as
a shrine. In the course of time all of Milton's eleven
places of residence in London disappeared.* During
September 2–5, 1666, Milton, back in Artillery Walk, was
on the edge of the Great Fire, an approximation to the
darker hell of his imagining.

* According to J. R. Martin (see above, footnote p. 58), this
was the pastel or crayon portrait (probably by Faithorne) that is
now at Princeton. Mr. Martin suggests (p. 12) that the anecdote
was amplified in transmission.

* A list of these may not be out of place. We have noted already
the destruction in the Great Fire of the old family house in Bread
Street, where Milton grew up. In 1640, after a short time in
lodgings in St. Bride's Churchyard, he took a house in Aldersgate
Street. About September, 1645, he moved to a house in the nearby
street called Barbican, running off from Aldersgate. In September–
October, 1647, he moved to a smaller house in High Holborn,
backing on Lincoln's Inn Fields. On his appointment as Secretary
(March, 1649) he took lodgings in a house at Charing Cross and
in November moved into the apartment in Scotland Yard, White-
hall, which had been assigned as his official residence. In December, 1651, Milton moved to a house in Petty France, Westminster,
"opening into St. James' Park." After the period of seclusion in
Bartholomew Close in the summer of 1660, Milton took a house
in Holborn, near Red Lion Fields. Perhaps early in 1661 he moved
to Jewin Street, near where he had lived in 1640–1647. In 1663,
not long after his third marriage (February), he settled in Artillery
Walk, Bunhill Fields, where he remained—except for the months
at Chalfont—until his death.

2

Paradise Lost

THE MANUSCRIPT of *Paradise Lost* Milton took with him to the country, where Ellwood, returning from a month in prison, read it (in August?), so that it must have been complete, whether or not it was revised in the next year and a half. The Plague and the Great Fire may have delayed publication. Some delay was caused by the licenser, the Reverend Thomas Tomkyns, who had frivolous objections, says Toland, and "would needs suppress the whole poem for imaginary treason" in the spacious and ominous simile (I.594–599) about the sun that

> In dim eclipse disastrous twilight sheds
> On half the nations, and with fear of change
> Perplexes monarchs.

The book was entered in the Stationers' Register on August 20, 1667, and published before the end of the year. It sold for three shillings. In April, 1667, Milton got £5 down, and a second £5, according to agreement, in April, 1669, when the first impression of thirteen hundred copies was exhausted; Milton's widow received £8 more in 1680, when the printer, Simmons, acquired full title to the work. The first edition comprised half a dozen issues dated 1667, 1668, and 1669; in the course of these Milton added the short preface in defense of blank verse and a prose "argument" for the whole poem. In its first form

it had ten books. In the second edition (1674) the seventh
and tenth books were each divided into two (a change
which somewhat shifted the final emphasis from man's
fall to his recovery), and a few lines were inserted as
beginnings for what were now the eighth and twelfth
books; some small changes were made; and the argument was split up into twelve parts placed at the head
of the respective books. In a commendatory poem Marvell
declared that his initial anxiety over Milton's project had
been wholly banished by the majestic result. This second
edition is the standard basis for modern texts, though
some actual or possible errors have to be corrected from
the first.

Milton's plan for an Arthurian epic, put forth in
Mansus and the *Epitaphium Damonis*, had apparently
been soon given up. The list of nearly a hundred biblical
and historical subjects for plays, which he set down
about 1640 in the Cambridge Manuscript, included four
drafts, of increasing fullness, for treatment of the story of
Adam and Eve in the semiallegorical vein of Italian
sacred drama. According to Edward Phillips, the first
part at least of Satan's address to the sun (*Paradise Lost*,
IV.32–41) was written very early as the opening speech
of a tragedy. We may suppose that Milton returned to
the epic because he shared the Renaissance veneration
for that as the supreme poetic form and because his
genius inclined to a panoramic sweep of narrative and
was cramped by dramatic limitations. The great work,
so long delayed, was to embody his total vision of life;
and the assertion of God's providence, though never in
doubt, was now far more difficult than it had been in
Lycidas. Scholarly guesses at the actual beginning of
the poem seem to favor 1657–1658, though some would
put it earlier. Certainly the heroic and moving passage
in the prelude to book seven was composed after the
Restoration:

Half yet remains unsung, but narrower bound
Within the visible diurnal sphere;
Standing on earth, not rapt above the pole,
More safe I sing with mortal voice, unchanged
To hoarse or mute, though fall'n on evil days,
On evil days though fall'n, and evil tongues;
In darkness, and with dangers compassed round,
And solitude. . . .

It seems a reasonable assumption, though some scholars would disagree, that Milton composed the poem mainly in its present sequence, for the sake of the imaginative momentum and structural ordering such a method would promote. At the same time, when we think of the extraordinary network of parallels and contrasts, especially the minute ones, and of many other refinements, we can hardly imagine that such a fabric "Rose like an exhalation," that it did not entail much recasting and revision.

In elaborating the meager data of Genesis, Milton had several large bodies of material to draw upon, and he did not have to get them up; his mind was full of them already, so that they flowed out freely, though always under firm control. The prime source was the whole Bible (including the Apocrypha), which he knew pretty much by heart; in addition to the central theme, it supplied endless allusions and words and phrases that carry significant overtones. There was also a mass of biblical and theological commentary old and new. Milton himself, in the 1640's, had begun making collections for what was to become his largest work and "my best and richest possession," *De Doctrina Christiana*, a comprehensive and critical summary of doctrine based strictly on the Bible. This treatise, which was virtually complete by about 1658–1660, is the most authoritative guide for the beliefs and ideas that constitute the bare bones of *Paradise Lost*. It spells out many things—among them Milton's late Arminianism and his heresies—that are less full or explicit in the poem; some ideas the poet seems to have modified. But, while in the theological as in every other area extraneous knowledge is helpful, the poem is always self-sufficient.

A third body of material comprised imaginative treatments of the creation and the fall written over many centuries. How many of these Milton knew we cannot tell, nor does it matter. Sylvester's flamboyant and popular rendering of Du Bartas's epic of creation, which Milton had echoed in his youth, would have less attraction for his mature taste (as for Dryden's); but the apparent borrowing of one line—"Immutable, immortal, infinite" (III.373)—is one reminder of the middlebrow reader's *Paradise Lost*. Milton probably knew two dramatic works which are somewhat closer to his own conception than most others, Grotius' *Adamus Exul* (1601) and Andreini's *L'Adamo* (1613). But, although the existence of many versions of the story meant that all had some family resemblance and that a good deal of Milton's plot was traditional, the fact has little to do with the masterful power of his re-creation, which stands alone. A poet treating the story was in much the same position as a Greek dramatist; he could build on general knowledge of his fable and its emotional associations while he reinterpreted it in accordance with his own vision. Also, Milton could go beyond epic predecessors in the large-scale use of dramatic irony, in the presentation of both Satan and his fellows and Adam and Eve. If the sacred character of a biblical theme imposed some limits, it did not forbid large and richly imaginative embellishments.

Many incidental embellishments might be adapted from the classical authors whom Milton had at his fingertips, such as the description in Plutarch's *Lycurgus* of the marching of Spartan soldiers (cf. *Paradise Lost*, I.549 f.). Both as sources for material and as models of structure there were the *Iliad* and *Odyssey*, which Milton was said

to have had by heart, and the *Aeneid*, the formal ideal of
neoclassical theory. He used and re-created, in strongly
functional ways, the standard conventions: the invocation of the Muse, the roll call of leaders, epic games, the
reported narrative of events that preceded the initial
plunge *in medias res*, verbal and physical battle, the
prophetic unfolding of history, and of course celestial
agencies.

While the classical epics stressed the hero's growth in
moral wisdom, a stress carried much further in *Paradise
Lost*, there was, after Homer, the difficulty of rendering
increasingly abstract themes in the concrete terms of epic
action. The philosophic Virgil came nearest Milton in his
doubly abstract theme, not only the moral growth of a
divinely guided hero but the divinely ordained mission
of Rome, yet this was more amenable to the Homeric
mold than a Christian poet's asserting of eternal Providence and justifying of God's ways to men. (There
is a further affinity, however remote, between Virgil
and Milton in that both deal with a "world destroyed and
world restored.") Then we may remember Milton's
saying—as Dryden recorded in his preface to the *Fables*—
that "Spenser was his original." That spacious remark—
which Humphrey Moseley had anticipated in regard to
Milton's early poems—may be taken to cover both poetic
artistry and the "sage and serious" Spenser's heroic and
figurative treatment of religious and moral ideas; in whatever ways Milton differed from or went beyond Spenser,
he was clearly of the same religious, cultural, and poetic
lineage.

In the prelude to book nine Milton repudiated traditional epic and romance in favor of his own "Not less but
more heroic" theme, and his transvaluation of epic values
operates throughout the poem. From the standpoint of
epic concreteness it may seem a fatal liability that the
dramatis personae are God, the Son, good and evil angels,

and the allegorical Sin and Death, and that there are no ordinary human characters until Adam and Eve become such in their fall. Yet this alleged liability is seldom felt. On the contrary, the supernatural and superhuman character of the fable makes and keeps it a grand archetypal myth—if that phrase can include both the Miltonic and the modern view of its fundamental and universal reality. Whatever reinterpretation a work of the past permits or demands, it must be understood first on its own terms as the product of a specific milieu, and a prime service of modern scholarship and criticism has been the re-creation of Milton's spiritual and intellectual world. We must read him as we read the ancients or Dante or Shakespeare, with imaginative sympathy for beliefs and assumptions that are not ours—and we may find that some of these are more valuable than our own, that we need readjustment more than the work in hand.

Paradise Lost would not be one of the supreme achievements of poetic imagination and art if it had not been fired by its author's intense and exalted religious faith. In the *Reason of Church Government* Milton had set forth, with his own special fervor, the Renaissance conception of poetry as "doctrinal and exemplary to a nation," as the teacher of religion and virtue. In telling his readers why he was forced to postpone his grand project, he had said that it was

a work not to be raised from the heat of youth or the vapors of wine, like that which flows at waste from the pen of some vulgar amorist or the trencher fury of a rhyming parasite; nor to be obtained by the invocation of Dame Memory and her siren daughters; but by devout prayer to that eternal Spirit who can enrich with all utterance and knowledge, and sends out his Seraphim with the hallowed fire of his altar to touch and purify the lips of whom he pleases.

Thus his appeals to the epic Muse, though remaining partly classical in form and texture, become earnest prayers for divine guidance. Milton the artist is a humble follower of the pagan ancients, but possession of Christian truth enables him "to soar Above th' Aonian mount," to sing "With other notes than to th' Orphean lyre." His first invocation links his Heavenly Muse (Urania, the Muse of astronomy, whom Renaissance poets had made the Muse of religious poetry) with that of Moses and with the creative power of God "brooding on the vast abyss" and suggests a parallel unfolding of huge events. The invocations that open books one, three, seven, and nine, and the somewhat different prelude to book four, signalize turning points in the narrative and changes of scene, sound the keynote, and establish the poet's authority; most of them are among the great things in the poem and in poetry. While expressing personal ideas and emotions, Milton is also dramatizing himself as the blind poet-prophet, who is one with

> Blind Thamyris and blind Maeonides,
> And Tiresias and Phineus prophets old.

Paradise Lost is neither a fundamentalist tract for Sunday reading nor a metaphysical inquiry into the origin and nature of evil but a "myth" about the actual and perpetual war between good and evil in the world and in the soul of man. In its total scheme it is a divine comedy, a tragic vision of human experience and history which ends with a measure of happiness and hope. It depicts the results of disobedience, of secular pride rebelling against the divine order, the order of love in harmony with law. Satan is the archetype of loveless pride, the egocentric lust for power; his reason and will are both corrupt. Adam and Eve were endowed with the free power of choice, "Sufficient to have stood, though free to fall." Eve sins through weakness of reason, Adam through weakness of will; both violate higher claims upon their love and conscience. But although they and their pos-

terity cannot, in a fallen and infected world, regain their
primal innocence and felicity, they can, through grace,
through love, through earnest effort, set their feet again
upon the right path, now with full knowledge of the conditions of human life. Such a bald summary, like a bald
summary of any complex vision, misses all the imaginative and artistic power that makes the poem a timeless
"emblem" of spiritual pride, anarchy, waste, despair, and
recovery. The outline has been put in terms that show
how alien the poem is to what we get, say, in much current fiction, the blend of toughness and sentimentalism
which modish reviewers like to call "religious"; if we take
that as the sum of wisdom and insight, we cannot respond
to Milton's blend of compassion with exacting ideals of
justice, righteousness, humility, and love—nor respond
even to his tremendous figure of the "Archangel ruined."
On the other hand, one strain in modern religious, imaginative, and critical writing has helped to create an atmosphere much more favorable to the sympathetic apprehen-
sion of Milton than the romantic and "liberal" tradition
of the nineteenth century allowed, that is, a renewed
understanding of pride, of the continual reenactment of
the fall, and even of grace.

The richly organic and dynamic pattern of the poem
must be largely taken for granted. Milton's physical universe is a mixture of the traditional and the imaginative:
between heaven at the top and hell at the bottom is
chaos, a vast raging sea of unformed elements; the newly
created world, the Ptolemaic world of ten spheres, hangs
by a golden chain from heaven and is very small in comparison with enveloping chaos and the total universe.
The Copernican theory, of which Milton showed some
knowledge, was not yet a wholly assured certainty
(Tycho Brahe's geocentric compromise Milton did not
refer to), and for a poet the Ptolemaic system, in addition
to its long and universal familiarity, had the advantage

of keeping the earth as a focal and stable center. The spatial structure, which is vertical and hierarchical, and the thematic structure coalesce in a way that is grandly simple in outline and subtly complex in depth and in detail. A fixed framework, with spatial and conceptual points of reference, provides a fixed criterion of value and at the same time provides for constant change and movement, ordered or disordered. Almost everyone and everything in the poem—"All but the throne itself of God"—is in movement, rising or falling, in a spiritual or a physical sense or both together.

In a short survey it seems best to stick closely to the fable, as if we were reading the poem for the first time and as if there were not a rapidly lengthening shelf of sophisticated critical studies. We can perhaps get at some things most readily by considering the main characters, and we may follow the order of their appearance on the cosmic stage.

It was a bold risk for Milton, intent on such a theme as his, to give his first two books, books of unflagging energy and splendor, to God's antagonist. Like Shakespeare (but with the epic poet's advantage of direct comment as well), Milton has his villains utter ideas that shock the moral and religious sense and thereby place the speaker. Satan's first speech, delivered to his lieutenant, Beelzebub, is a grand defiance of God, a superlative piece of rhetoric in which every phrase reveals his false scale of values, his unconquerable will and immortal hate, his egoistic pride and passion. It inaugurates the dramatic irony in which Satan and his followers are enveloped throughout. So too in his third speech (I.242 f.) Satan the prisoner in hell proclaims himself its "new possessor"; utters a mainly false boast—later to be bitterly retracted—that

> The mind is its own place, and in itself
> Can make a heav'n of hell, a hell of heav'n;

and shows again his egoistic pride in declaring that

> To reign is worth ambition, though in hell:
> Better to reign in hell than serve in heav'n.

If the modern reader does not share Milton's conception of God, "whose service is perfect freedom," presumably he has some abstract ideal of order and good, and that may serve as a criterion. The God whom Satan denounces as a lucky general with heavier armament is an absolute which cannot possibly be overthrown, so that the devils' plots and acts are futile products of corruption and blindness. While Satan assuredly compasses the fall of man, he cannot extinguish goodness in him, much less the divine principle of good.

Moving from the fiery lake to the fiery shore, the "great Sultan" (a seventeenth-century equivalent of Führer or Commissar) rallies his prostrate legions and, in a passage rich in exotic and significant associations, Milton gives a roll call of the leaders, who are seen as the future gods of debased heathenism. There follows the martial pageantry of a review, a spectacle that arouses both pride and remorse in the commander. Here Satan, who embodies on a superhuman scale all the merely heroic qualities of the classical epic hero, has a greatness or grandeur that can be measured only in terms of the sun in eclipse and scars of thunder (I.589 f.). Throughout the early books, though Satan's evil character is manifest from the start, we share the degree of imaginative sympathy that enabled Milton, *qua* poet, to create one of the supreme figures of world literature; a part of our mind is greatly stirred, on the principle Keats cited from Hazlitt (without reference to Satan), that we "read with pleasure of the ravages of a beast of prey" because of "the sense of power abstracted from the sense of good."

The fallen angels build Pandemonium, that florid substitute for the courts of heaven, and Satan, "High on a throne of royal state," calls for a discussion of policy. The rhetorical virtuosity and the realism of Milton's debate dwarf the dozens of councils in earlier epics (indeed his long practice in the arts of persuasion shows itself in every speech in the poem). The speakers characterize themselves in their ideas and style—Moloch, the simple-minded, saber-rattling general whose "sentence is for open war," Belial, the smooth diplomat and intellectual, Mammon, for whom the gold of hell is equivalent to heaven. And they all evoke tacit responses in their audience to point after point of fallacious argument. Many readers have felt that Milton's success owed much to his close concern with public affairs (not that members of parliament or the Council of State shared diabolic sentiments). One realistic bit of business is that, after speakers have held forth from the floor, Beelzebub, as Satan had arranged, proposes that they seek revenge on God by corrupting his new creation. Satan alone has the courage to volunteer for the mission, and he fully exploits its perils, for his greater glory. His followers now indulge in "epic games," but their athletic and martial contests, their heroic songs and philosophic debates, are all futile busyness, a pathetic travesty of heavenly order and an anticipation of much of the activity of fallen mankind. Their blind anarchy and despair are symbolized in the physical character of the hell they explore,

Rocks, caves, lakes, fens, bogs, dens, and shades of death,
A universe of death. . . .

Satan, setting forth on his quest, is challenged at the gates of hell by the grisly monsters Sin and Death. Sin had, like Athene, sprung from his head when he first conceived of rebellion, and Death is the offspring of his dalliance with her (James, 1:15). This unique allegorical episode (to be continued in book ten) is a potent reminder of the heroic Satan's real nature and is still more potent as a hideous parody of the Trinity: Sin looks forward to the time when "I shall reign At thy right hand voluptuous" (one cannot miss the shock of the retarded epithet). Satan, with undaunted strength, makes his way up through the warring elements of chaos until he lands on the top of the created world (the Ptolemaic world with the earth at its center), which is suspended from heaven. Gliding down through spheres and stars, he alights on the sun, deceives its angelic guardian, and reaches the earth. Here, addressing the sun, whose hateful light recalls what once he was, Satan utters his first soliloquy (IV. 32 f.), a grim contrast with the poet's invocation to Light which had opened book three. No longer haranguing his followers, Satan admits all his wickedness, and he reminds us of Faustus as "conscience wakes despair"; "Which way I fly is hell; myself am hell." But, unable to repent, he ends with the resolve, "Evil, be thou my good." Satan's tortured conscience, which sets him apart from all his fellows, gives him new and tragic dimensions, but his tragic potentialities—unlike Macbeth's —are never allowed to develop. As he approaches his goal, a succession of similes—of a vulture, a wolf, a robber—and his own speeches reinforce our sense of the character and motives which his strong and glamorous leadership in hell had partly disguised.

When in the garden Satan, in the form of a cormorant, beholds Adam and Eve, another soliloquy reveals his envy and self-pity. In the sardonic vein of Richard III or Iago, he gloats over the fate he has in store for them, and (with an echo of Isaiah, 14:9) wit swells into spacious poetry:

> Hell shall unfold,
> To entertain you two, her widest gates,
> And send forth all her kings.

Taking various animal shapes, for closer approach, Satan learns from Adam's talk with Eve of the forbidden tree of knowledge of good and evil and is provided with a plan of campaign. At night the good angels find him "Squat like a toad, close at the ear of Eve," instilling into her

> Vain hopes, vain aims, inordinate desires
> Blown up with high conceits engend'ring pride.

Raphael's long narrative of Satan's revolt and the war in heaven deepens the picture of his egoism and falsity: his envy of the Son's elevation (like Macbeth's at Duncan's naming his son Prince of Cumberland), his deceitful seduction of his followers into rebellion, his argument with the righteous Abdiel, the appearance of "Th' Apostate in his sun-bright chariot" as an "Idol of majesty divine," and his display in battle of both the resource and the cynical wit of the professional soldier.

Book nine brings us back to the present and to the tragic climax. In a midnight soliloquy (contrasted with the earlier address to the sun) Satan is wholly committed to evil, prideful spite against God and man mingling with a self-pity aggravated by his "foul descent" into a serpent's body. In the morning he finds Eve alone and of course achieves his end. When she has succumbed, "Back to the thicket slunk The guilty serpent." We see no more of him until, in his own form, he is returning to hell and again meets Sin and Death, who have built a bridge to the world that is now part of their dominion; and we have again a travesty of God and the Son, as if the making of the bridge were the creation of that world. Satan reenters Pandemonium with "the dictator's flair for the theatrical" and reports his triumph. *Hubris* brings on nemesis, a more than Ovidian transformation: applause turns into hissing as Satan and his fellows are all changed into serpents. The bestial mask has become a wholesale actuality. Yet evil, though ultimately self-destructive, has begun its work on earth.

Milton's God has incurred strong censure, some perhaps legitimate, some merely wrongheaded. Much of the latter kind has in the past rested on the naïve choice of Satan as the authoritative guide to Milton's theology and total conception—as if we should read *Othello* or *King Lear* from the standpoint of Iago or Edmund. It may have been a strategic error to make God a speaking character, though it is hard to see how in such a fable, cast in the concrete heroic mold, that could have been avoided; at any rate, if in a few places God speaks like Milton the pamphleteer, at other times he speaks like a Deity. The "unpoetical" bareness of his language may be ascribed to the poet's reverent feeling that the speech of Truth must be unadorned. For Coleridge, Milton "was very wise in adopting the strong anthropomorphism of the Hebrew Scriptures at once," and his judgment "in the conduct of the celestial part of this story is very exquisite." Since Coleridge's perceptions are of singular value, we may note also his opinion that in the "combination of poetry with doctrines . . . Dante has not succeeded . . . nearly so well as Milton."*

Although the poem has often been labeled "the Puritan epic," the Puritanism in it is an almost invisible tincture found only in two or three incidental bits. Some main charges against Milton's God are only charges against the Christian God, whose least attractive attribute, derived from Reformation theology, Milton emphatically rejects. When in the third book the poet moves up from hell to heaven, from the infernal to the celestial council, the invocation to Light fills our minds with a renewed sense of God as infinite Spirit, the source of all being and all good. Then God expounds the nature and destiny of man and, in part, his own nature: he has given reason and free will to man, who is responsible for his own fate.

* *Coleridge on the Seventeenth Century*, ed. Roberta F. Brinkley (Duke University Press, 1955), pp. 590-591, 598.

Continuing his repudiation of Calvinism, God defines the "elect" in the Arminian sense: they are not a predestined few but all believers. Yet justice is justice and may not be violated without the collapse of the moral universe, and man's "Affecting Godhead" is a sin that must be paid for:

> He with his whole posterity must die;
> Die he or justice must; unless for him
> Some other able, and as willing, pay
> The rigid satisfaction, death for death.

No doubt many readers recoil from such ideas of sin, guilt, and justice as stark Puritan legalism. But there is nothing peculiarly Puritan in the conception, as one of countless witnesses, Bishop Lancelot Andrewes, may remind us:

Fond men! if He would quit His justice or waive His truth, He could; but His justice and truth are to Him as essential, as intrinsically essential, as His mercy; of equal regard, every way as dear to Him. Justice otherwise remains unsatisfied; and satisfied it must be either on Him or on us.*

If the Christian tradition leaves us cold, we may remember the sternly unsentimental conception of Justice, *Dike*, which was central in Greek religious thought and tragic drama. In the Graeco-Roman-Christian tradition of Christian humanism, of which Hooker and Milton are classic exemplars, God is among other things the source and guarantee of order, of absolutes which he himself could not alter; he is not Calvin's arbitrary and inscrutable Will but Reason and Will, Moral Law. Even if Milton's God were presented with the compelling imaginative force of Satan (which no poet could achieve), he would still be antipathetic to an age that has changed "sinful" to "antisocial." Whatever our naturalistic condi-

* *XCVI Sermons* (1629), p. 101; *Ninety-Six Sermons* (Oxford, 1841), I, 184–185.

tioning may have been, we cannot read Milton—as we cannot read Shakespeare—without an active sense of a divine order. And, when we remember the militant revolutionist's hopes, we feel both sublimity and pathos in his recurrent anticipations of their fulfillment only after the judgment day:

> The world shall burn, and from her ashes spring
> New heav'n and earth, wherein the just shall dwell,
> And after all their tribulations long
> See golden days, fruitful of golden deeds,
> With joy and love triumphing, and fair truth.
> Then thou thy regal scepter shalt lay by,
> For regal scepter then no more shall need;
> God shall be all in all.   (III.334 f.)

For the most metaphysical conception of God in the poem we may move up to his speech delivered as he sends forth the Son to create the world (VII.168 f.):

> Boundless the deep, because I am who fill
> Infinitude, nor vacuous the space.
> Though I uncircumscribed myself retire,
> And put not forth my goodness, which is free
> To act or not, Necessity and Chance
> Approach not me, and what I will is Fate.

The "I" is pure Being, and "what I will" is the rational order of the universe, what Hooker calls "that order which God before all ages hath set down with himself, for himself to do all things by." Though God permeates all space, he has not hitherto exerted his creative power upon chaos, but he now does so, voluntarily, and his acts are not subject to the necessity or chance of pagan or modern philosophies. In the *Christian Doctrine* Milton opposed the orthodox view that God created the world out of nothing and argued that he created it out of his own substance (a view which, in Christian tradition, seems to have begun with Gregory of Nyssa and pseudo-

Dionysius); but the reinterpretative language of the poem does not directly challenge orthodoxy. However, while the metaphysical theology is essential, the most imaginative depiction of the Deity is in descriptive passages where the God-intoxicated poet feels and excites "an hypnosis of awe"—"Dark with excessive bright thy skirts appear."

The Son, the "Word," is God's deputy in the war in heaven, in the creation, in the judgment of Adam and Eve, and is of course the agent of man's redemption. In the council in heaven, in book three, when God appeals for "Some other," the Son volunteers to be the sacrifice justice requires for man—as Satan was the sole volunteer for man's destruction. The Son is the divine hero of the poem, Adam the earthly one; the second Adam regains what the first Adam lost. Throughout, the Son's "merit," his love, humility, and right reason are opposed to the "merit," hate, pride, and passion of Satan. The Son is the voice of love and mercy and his speeches embody a special and recognizable rhythm. The speaking roles of God and the Son provide some celestial drama, although, in dividing the attributes of Deity, they can have the effect of making God seem harsh. Epic anthropomorphism may also seem to give a dynastic tinge to religious symbolism, as when, at the chronological beginning of the story, in the act that incites Satan to revolt, God, echoing Psalm 2:6–7, proclaims the Son, this day begotten, as his vicegerent (V.600 f.); what it means is that the Son is now established as king and mediator, as the active force of good. The most notorious heresy in Milton's *Christian Doctrine* is his "Arianism" (a creed he had condemned in his early tracts); perhaps the term should be modified to "anti-Trinitarianism." At any rate, although *Paradise Lost* awakened few misgivings in generations of devoutly orthodox readers, its presentation of the Son, "of all creation first," is nowhere incompatible with the denial in the treatise of his co-equality with the Father. In his subordination of the Son, Milton was in accord with most of the ante-Nicene Fathers of the church.

For the overthrow of the rebel angels and the work of creation the Son is invested with paternal powers. The Bible gave only hints for the war (Isaiah, 14:12 f.; 2 Peter, 2:4; Jude, 6; Rev. 12:4, 7-9), but theological tradition, the mythological wars of gods, Titans and giants, and Milton's imagination supplied the rest. His handling of the battles has been thought too unrealistic for an epic and too realistic for a symbol, and the earlier stages are perhaps too much spun out. But the poet's energy is abundant and the range of significance is wide, from the immediate rendering of Satan's anarchic passion and violence (which is a lesson for Adam) to the monstrous confusion and waste of human wars and perhaps a typological foreshadowing of Armageddon and the second coming of Christ. Above all there is the climactic picture of the representative of absolute order and good sent out to end the conflict:

> Forth rushed with whirlwind sound
> The chariot of Paternal Deity,
> Flashing thick flames. . . .

> Attended with ten thousand thousand saints,
> He onward came, far off his coming shone. . . .

The rebel angels are driven through the opened wall of heaven and fall for nine days and nights into the pit of hell—the point at which the poem had begun.

Upon the wild anarchy of war there follows the great work of peace, the creation of the world and a new race of beings. The description of the Son, endued with God's "overshadowing spirit and might," going forth to perform the work (VII.205-220) is a magnificent example of Milton's suggestive visual images, his sense of vast space, and his expressive manipulation of rhythm, and, in its imposing of order, the passage stands in contrast with Satan's flight through chaos:

> Heav'n opened wide
> Her ever-during gates, harmonious sound
> On golden hinges moving, to let forth
> The King of Glory in his powerful Word
> And Spirit coming to create new worlds.
> On heav'nly ground they stood, and from the shore
> They viewed the vast immeasurable abyss
> Outrageous as a sea, dark, wasteful, wild,
> Up from the bottom turned by furious winds
> And surging waves, as mountains to assault
> Heav'n's highth, and with the center mix the pole.
>   "Silence, ye troubled waves, and thou deep, peace,"
> Said then th' omnific Word, "your discord end."
>   Nor stayed, but on the wings of Cherubim
> Uplifted, in paternal glory rode
> Far into Chaos and the world unborn. . . .

The elaborate account of creation, partly imagined, partly gathered from heterogeneous sources, is alive with light and color, movement and growth. Milton is too wholehearted a Christian, and too monistic a metaphysician, to feel an antithesis between the Many and the One, between the mackerel-crowded seas and the city of Byzantium. For him nature is the art of God, and the plenitude and variety of creation manifest the divine power and goodness, the vitality and glory, the "enormous bliss," of an innocent world. His imagination is excited, as always, by the fecundity of terrestrial nature, "Wild above rule or art" (V.297), and no less by the majestic order of the planets, the "starry dance." Creation "Answering his great Idea" (the last word, which occurs nowhere else in Milton's poetry, links Plato with Hebraic and Christian tradition), the Son returns to heaven (VII.557 f.):

                    Up he rode
Followed with acclamation and the sound
Symphonious of ten thousand harps that tuned
Angelic harmonies. The earth, the air
Resounded (thou remember'st, for thou heard'st).
The heav'ns and all the constellations rung,
The planets in their stations list'ning stood,
While the bright pomp ascended jubilant.

"In the last line," Sir Walter Raleigh remarked, "the first
four words marshal the great procession in solid array;
the last two lift it high into the empyrean."

Adam and Eve are, like Satan, enveloped in irony, but
through innocence and human weakness, not self-
engendered depravity. It was a major stroke of irony for
Milton to withhold his picture of idyllic paradise and its
idyllic inhabitants until we accompany Satan into the
garden and see its pastoral and human glories under the
shadow of his presence. Milton pours into his description
all the traditional elements of earthly paradises and the
golden age. Mythological images add their ideal and
nostalgic radiance, among them that most beautiful and
poignant of all similes, which suggests both the fate of
Eve and the transiency of all earthly beauty:

                    Not that fair field
Of Enna, where Prosérpine gathering flow'rs,
Herself a fairer flow'r, by gloomy Dis
Was gathered, which cost Ceres all that pain
To seek her through the world.

The whole richly stylized picture gives, not the physical
sensation of a garden, but a symbolic vision of perfection, and Adam and Eve, like their surroundings, are kept
at an aesthetic distance; otherwise they would be a pair
of suburban nudists. They are ideal man and woman, in
the full happiness of mutual love and harmony with God
and nature; and that harmony is reflected in the gracious

elevation of their speech. A signal example is Eve's asseveration of her love for Adam (IV.641–656), a pastoral hymn in which she weaves and unweaves an elaborate pattern of images.

Adam and Eve posed an artistic problem: they must be sinless, yet sin, when it comes, must seem logical, not a sudden and unaccountable lapse. Preparation for the fall begins in Eve's first speech (IV. 440 f.), her story of her first experience of being alive. Seeing her face in a pool, she had loved it, and when she turned away at her first sight of Adam, he followed, crying "Return, fair Eve, Whom fli'st thou?" As Eve recalls Narcissus, Adam recalls Apollo's pursuit of Daphne (both Ovidian tales); while these acts are wholly natural and blameless, they give faint hints of Eve's possible self-centeredness and Adam's possibly excessive devotion. A much stronger hint soon develops. Satan's efforts at Eve's ear resulted in her dreaming that, guided as she thought by Adam and then by an angel, she ate of the forbidden fruit and felt exalted like a god (V.86 f.). Now, waking, she rejoices that it was only a bad dream, and Adam ministers psychiatric comfort; yet the pattern has taken shape in her mind and in ours. "So all was cleared, and to the field they haste." Their morning prayer, sadly ironic by anticipation, is a canticle which starts from Psalm 148, in praise of God's wondrous creation. It is a microcosm, on the "good" side, of the whole poem: everything from sun and moon to the song of birds is in harmonious movement, rising or falling.

The angel Raphael is sent from heaven (as Virgil had Mercury sent to Dido) to instruct Adam and Eve and give them a last warning. A vegetarian picnic and the problem of angelic digestion lead into the Renaissance doctrine of cosmic order, the great chain of being (V.414 f., 469 f.). But this goes beyond the ideas most familiar in Ulysses' speech in *Troilus and Cressida* (I.iii), for Raphael sets forth a metaphysical monism, a denial of any essential difference between matter and spirit. All things are "one first matter," all proceeding from and returning to God, "If not depraved from good." Matter is thus inherently good and in its various forms and degrees is in a perpetual process of becoming, "Till body up to spirit work, in bounds Proportioned to each kind"; human bodies "may at last turn all to spirit, Improved by tract of time."

Raphael then launches upon his narrative of earlier events, with the first of several significant apologies for "lik'ning spiritual to corporal forms." The story of Satan's revolt against the divine order shows "By terrible example the reward Of disobedience," and the story of creation glorifies the happy lot of man, created in God's image to enjoy God's world. Book eight is a large link in the preparation for the fall. In answer to Adam's question, an old one about cosmic economy, Raphael presents the alternative theories of a geocentric or heliocentric universe and the possibility of other inhabited worlds, but what he stresses is the danger of merely speculative curiosity concerning things external and remote:

> Solicit not thy thoughts with matters hid:
> Leave them to God alone, him serve and fear.

Some critics, recalling Milton's emphasis on science in *Of Education* and on free inquiry in *Areopagitica*, have charged him with obscurantism here. But it is a matter of motive and degree. At the beginning of the second book of the *Reason of Church Government* Milton had distinguished between the "lower wisdom" of natural science and "the only high valuable wisdom" of the religious and righteous life. Among the century's many available witnesses on this point, one is Ralph Cudworth, the Cambridge Platonist, in his great sermon to the House of Commons on March 31, 1647:

We think it a gallant thing to be fluttering up to heaven with our wings of knowledge and speculation: whereas the highest mystery of a divine life here, and of perfect happiness hereafter, consisteth in nothing but mere obedience to the divine will.

Dr. Johnson, deprecating Milton's emphasis on science in education, said that "we are perpetually moralists, but we are geometricians only by chance"—which, so far as it goes, is Milton's own position. He is not condemning science or astronomy *per se* (*Paradise Lost* includes tributes to Galileo), but any preoccupation with secondary things that obscures the prime ends of life; and we in the second half of the twentieth century can hardly afford to feel complacent about all the results of science or to blame the many seventeenth-century men who put first things first. We may note, incidentally, that Milton (like most men of his and earlier times) was not troubled by the Copernican theory or even by the idea of a plurality of inhabited worlds. He is not appalled by the silence of infinite space; God's omnipresence removes any thought of fear.

In the second half of book eight Adam describes his first experience of life. The major premise here is the universal doctrine of hierarchical order, in particular Adam's place in the chain of being. In his picture of nuptial love sanctified by God and nature Adam avows the strange power of passion, and his eulogy of Eve (546–559) becomes such an abdication of his own dignity and responsibility that it draws a rebuke from Raphael. Romantic sentimentalists resent the rebuke and the angel's subordination of the flesh to love founded in reason and religion. But Milton had earlier (IV.741 f.) glorified physical union; here he is stressing Adam's need of integrity. At first sight this half of book eight may seem remote from the astronomical half, but in fact they are closely related: they show how man violates the hierarchy of values if he lets either intellectual pride or idolatry of a creature become his ultimate principle and allegiance.

When Raphael departs, with a final warning, Adam and Eve are on their own. Hitherto they have been presented as personages in act and utterance above the human level, as figures in a divinely harmonious order. Now aesthetic distance gives place to close-up drama (such as no earlier epic had developed) and the ceremony of innocence to realistic feelings and speech— though we are never allowed to forget what they have been; indeed, to the rational and religious theme of moral choice a further emotional dimension is added by Milton's nostalgic ideal of unfallen perfection.* Only an outline, however inadequate, can suggest the really dramatic handling of the fall, the very human mixture of right and wrong in both Adam and Eve and the mixture of sympathy and justice in Milton.

Eve's proposal that they work apart, so as not to spend time in dalliance, evokes Adam's praise for her zeal but also a warning of the danger that threatens them and of her need for his protective presence. The implied reflection on her strength draws from her the first note of human, feminine shrillness, and "domestic" Adam says, with belated tact, that they support each other. But Eve urges with vigor the sufficiency of virtue and the merit of resisting evil. She is not upholding what Milton had said in *Areopagitica*, in regard to the fallen world, about "a fugitive and cloistered virtue . . . that never sallies out and sees her adversary"; she, in a sinless world, is aggressively asserting herself, inviting trouble, putting a bit of work before her relations with Adam and before the

* E.g., IV.222, 317–318, 774–775, VII.631–632, XI.88–89. The third and fourth of these items echo Virgil's praise of the humble Italian farmers who shun urban ambitions (*Georg.* II.458 f.), a passage we shall meet again.

mode of life designed by the Creator. (Adam had shown
—though without persisting—a touch of the same spirit
when he questioned the order the Creator appointed for
the cosmos and the relations of man and wife.) Adam
reminds her of what may (and does) happen, that her
reason may mislead her will into disobedience; but he
surrenders, and Eve, withdrawing her hand from his,
goes off in her pride and beauty "like a wood-nymph
light." The ambiguous "light" suggests both physical
grace and mental unawareness. The poet's compassion is
expressed directly and then in the picture of her among
the flowers which, molded in the same pattern as the
earlier allusion to Proserpine, now openly anticipates her
imminent fall:

> . . . them she upstays
> Gently with myrtle band, mindless the while,
> Herself, though fairest unsupported flow'r,
> From her best prop so far, and storm so nigh.

The serpent—Satan in the serpent—happily finds the
weaker victim alone; overpowered by her loveliness, he
is for the moment "Stupidly good, of enmity disarmed."
Satan addresses Eve with flattery and, when she is
surprised by his ability to speak, he tells her of the wondrous fruit that gave him high powers. The "unwary"
and "credulous" Eve follows his lead, but recoils when
they come to the forbidden tree. Satan utters a vehement
protest on behalf of man, who would enjoy godlike
knowledge if he were not kept ignorant by a jealous
Deity, and in a soliloquy Eve accepts all his specious
arguments on behalf of her injured merit.

> So saying, her rash hand in evil hour
> Forth reaching to the fruit, she plucked, she eat.
> Earth felt the wound, and Nature from her seat
> Sighing through all her works gave signs of woe,
> That all was lost.

Eve quickly reaches a state of *hubris,*

> through expectation high
> Of knowledge, nor was Godhead from her thought.
> Greedily she engorged without restraint,
> And knew not eating death.

Her next soliloquy reveals her complete corruption. She rejoices in having attained godlike elevation, in spite of "Our great Forbidder" and his spies. Thinking aloud —not with the majestic speech of innocence and familiar certainties but in phrases that explore the new world of sin—she proceeds to selfish calculation, whether to share her knowledge with Adam or keep it to herself,

> so to add what wants
> In female sex, the more to draw his love,
> And render me more equal, and perhaps,
> A thing not undesirable, sometime
> Superior; for inferior who is free?

Thus she has arrived at Satan's view of freedom as self-assertive power. But what if God punish her with death and Adam wed another Eve?

> Adam shall share with me in bliss or woe.
> So dear I love him, that with him all deaths
> I could endure, without him live no life.

Such words are sincere self-deception.

Paying to the tree the reverence she denies to God, Eve returns, carrying a bough of fruit, and is met by the anxious Adam, who has come to meet her with a garland of flowers he has woven for her hair. With "count'nance blithe" and flushed, and with lies about her supreme concern for him, Eve describes, in terms of *hubris,* the effects of the fruit. Adam in horror drops his faded garland and breaks out in words which mingle right-minded love with that idolatrous excess for which he had been rebuked by Raphael:

O fairest of creation, last and best
Of all God's works, creature in whom excelled
Whatever can to sight or thought be formed,
Holy, divine, good, amiable, or sweet!
How art thou lost, how on a sudden lost,
Defaced, deflow'red, and now to death devote!

And he goes on to a cry of anguish at the thought of
idyllic Eden as a desert without her:

How can I live without thee, how forgo
Thy sweet converse and love so dearly joined,
To live again in these wild woods forlorn?

After the first shock, Adam argues that perhaps Eve's sin
is not fatal, and he repeats his resolve to share her doom,
whatever it may be. In modern writing we are usually
expected to applaud the supreme claims of any human
love, regardless of all other claims; Milton expects us to
share his own heartfelt sympathy, but also to see what
Adam does not see. For that we might borrow the words
of Jane Eyre:

My future husband was becoming to me my whole world;
and more than the world: almost my hope of heaven. He
stood between me and every thought of religion, as an
eclipse intervenes between man and the broad sun. I could
not, in those days, see God for his creature: of whom I had
made an idol.

If religious criteria leave us unmoved, we may remember
that, because we sympathize with the fleeing Hector and
the adulterous Helen, we do not abandon our higher
belief in courage and fidelity; or, in the political sphere,
we recognize the total betrayal of principle in the doctrine "My country, right or wrong."

If Adam has the real but inadequate virtue of human
loyalty, Eve remains largely self-centered. Her response
to Adam's declaration begins "O glorious trial of exceed-
ing love," an unconsciously ironic reminder of Christ's

selfless love for man. Eve in sinning had let her weak reason and conscience be misled by an apparent good; Adam lets his will be oversway ed by devotion to her:

> He scrupled not to eat
> Against his better knowledge, not deceived,
> But fondly overcome with female charm.

The effects of the completed sin are quickly manifest: the pair who had visions of achieving superhuman knowledge and power sink to subhuman lust. Adam's invitation to Eve displays a callous sensual levity reinforced by echoes of Paris's speech to Helen and Zeus's to Hera in the third and fourteenth books of the *Iliad:*

> For never did thy beauty since the day
> I saw thee first and wedded thee, adorned
> With all perfections, so inflame my sense
> With ardor to enjoy thee, fairer now
> Than ever, bounty of this virtuous tree.

After the mutual love and reverence of earlier scenes, we get a dramatic shock from the brutality of "enjoy thee." And when we think of the clasped hands of those scenes, there is another shock in "Her hand he seized. . . ." Before, their nuptial bower and nuptial rites had symbolized their purity; now, the flowers of their casual bed are still pure, though they are not. When they waken after their sport, Adam is overcome with guilt, with the loss of his old joy in the presence of God or angel. Their resort to banyan leaves is an admission of their fallen, indeed savage, state. In their minds the hierarchy of faculties has become chaos and passions rule. Quarreling and blaming each other, the regal pair are now the wholly and merely human Mr. and Mrs. John Doe.

In book ten the Son, after addressing the Father in his characteristic accents of love, comes down to judge the sinners, blending justice with tender mercy. But the eternal spring and the beauty of Eden, the primal con-

cord of the beasts, turn into the harsh and warring world
of actuality. Adam, in a long and despairing soliloquy,
tries in vain to assert the injustice of the fate he has
brought on himself and his descendants:

> On the ground
> Outstretched he lay, on the cold ground, and oft
> Cursed his creation. . . .

Longing for death, he recalls the songs of praise he had
once uttered to woods and fountains, hillocks, dales, and
bowers. In his rage against himself he fiercely denounces
Eve. She, whose thoughts have been left to our imagining, now initiates good as she had initiated evil. She falls
weeping at his feet and speaks in that minor key—heard
usually on the lips of the Son—that is the voice of love:

> Forsake me not thus, Adam, witness Heav'n
> What love sincere and reverence in my heart
> I bear thee, and unweeting have offended,
> Unhappily deceived; thy suppliant
> I beg, and clasp thy knees; bereave me not
> Whereon I live, thy gentle looks, thy aid,
> Thy counsel in this uttermost distress,
> My only strength and stay.

Reconciliation brings them closer together, on the farther
side of the vale of experience, than they were in their
idyllic state. Eve goes on, with a boldness that startles
Adam, to propose that they blunt the judgment pronounced on their progeny by either abstaining from
intercourse—

> which would be misery
> And torment less than none of what we dread—

or by committing suicide. But Eve, in happiness or in
misery, is always more concerned about Adam and the
here and now than about God, and Adam's higher in-

sight tells her that their only real resource is in humble and prayerful penitence. However woeful their plight, these human creatures, aided by grace, are now engendering a force of good that can stand against evil. Book nine had ended with quarreling; book ten ends with the poetry—it is poetry—of "hearts contrite."

Feeling happier, Adam and Eve look forward to life in Eden, "though in fall'n state, content," but the angel Michael comes to tell them they must leave the paradise they have forfeited. Their reactions are typical: Eve is the housewife who must abandon her home, Adam is afflicted in being hidden from the face of God—though Michael, speaking in the rhythm of love, assures him that God is everywhere. Michael then fulfills his further mission, the presenting to Adam, in vision and narrative, of the future history of mankind. But his revelation, far from Anchises' inspiring picture of the destiny of Rome, shows "supernal grace contending With sinfulness of men." Although the seeds of goodness in Adam and Eve will in the course of time flower in some rare spirits, history, from Cain onward, is mainly a story of evil. These last two books have often been slighted as a dull appendage, but they are an integral part of Milton's total theme: for both Adam and the reader they translate into historical actuality the parable of the fall, a renewal of hell on earth; they explain the means of redemption, human and divine; and they have drama in the often mistaken reactions of Adam's as yet only half-enlightened mind. The story embodies a pessimism that only invincible faith in Providence can surmount. The fallen world is one of crime, disease and decay, licentiousness, oppression, war—

> So all shall turn degenerate, all depraved,
> Justice and temperance, truth and faith forgot.

Noah's flood is only a temporary cleansing, though book
eleven ends with the covenant symbolized by the
rainbow.

After a pause "Betwixt the world destroyed and world
restored" Michael continues the tale of human wickedness. True liberty, which always with right reason dwells,
is lost, in individual men and in nations (the coupling
recalls Plato's *Republic*). Out of the gloomy context rises
one triumphant passage (XII.285–306), on the super-
seding of Mosaic law, the covenant of works, by Christian liberty, a passage in which ideas, profoundly felt,
become great poetry. The most indifferent reader can
hardly fail to respond to what B. Rajan has finely described as "the massive and moving finality with which
Milton sums up the relationship of the Gospel to the
Law . . . the severe yet ardent splendour of those antith-
eses, the upsurge of joyousness that moves in Milton's
mind when he celebrates the union of discipline with
freedom."[*]

The story moves rapidly to the Incarnation and Crucifixion, the grand conquest of evil, and finally to the day
of judgment and eternity. Thus enlightened, Adam (in
terms of a traditional paradox) can wonder if his fall was
not fortunate, since it set in motion the power of exemplary and redemptive love. Yet Michael goes on to
describe the corruption of Christianity itself in lines
(especially XII.535 f.) that might seem to leave no
ground for hope. In the end Adam is able to affirm
a truly religious faith, the humble and obedient heroism
which alone can overcome Satan; and his statement, like
some other purely religious passages, is poetry. Michael
replies, "This having learnt, thou hast attained the sum
Of wisdom," and at this climactic point he recalls that
central theme, the difference between mere knowledge,

[*] *Paradise Lost & The Seventeenth Century Reader* (London:
Chatto & Windus, 1947), p. 90.

a potential source of intellectual pride, and the Christian and classical virtues, the soul of which is love. If he possesses these, Adam, though exiled from paradise, will have an inward paradise, happier far.

Now "all in bright array The Cherubim descended" to expel Adam and Eve into the world of history to begin life anew. They look back at what was "so late their happy seat,"

> Waved over by that flaming brand, the gate
> With dreadful faces thronged and fiery arms.
> Some natural tears they dropped, but wiped them soon;
> The world was all before them, where to choose
> Their place of rest, and Providence their guide:
> They hand in hand, with wand'ring steps and slow,
> Through Eden took their solitary way.

Of all Milton's perfect endings this is the most wonderful in its simplicity of texture and complexity of meaning. He does not now have the militant, half-mundane vision with which he had ended his first tract, when he had seen Christ returning to reward religious and patriotic leaders with "the regal additions of principalities, legions, and thrones into their glorious titles. . . ." The picture of Everyman and Everywoman is a final "emblem" of life in human and Christian terms: every phrase is set off against other phrases, so that all create the most compassionate and poignant blend of sorrow, fear, loneliness, comradeship, faith, and hope.

Some parallels and contrasts in scene and action, character and theme, have been noted, and the whole fabric is bound together by contrasts, large and small, between good and evil, love and hate, life and death, humility and pride, reason and passion, order and anarchy, liberty and servitude, nature and artifice, harmony and dissonance, and so on. In the way of visual imagery the most important thread of contrast is between light and dark-

ness, and "holy Light" is identified with all good, from
God and the Son down to "the bright consummate flow'r."
Evil is identified with the lurid darkness or false glitter
of hell, and the first book is full of pictures that suggest
the strength and corruption, the dignity and degradation,
of the damned: Satan rising from the lake of fire and
moving shoreward, standing on the beach and calling his
legions; the resplendent banners and arms of the troops
marching before their leader; the overrich architecture
of Pandemonium. Whether in hell or heaven or inter-
stellar space, generalized terms—completely different
from Dante's minute particularity—establish norms or
create magnitude, distance, horror, sublimity. Abstrac-
tions are an element in the poem's mythic character. Yet
the vague and abstract have enough of the concrete to
give the Miltonic universe, for all its vastness and un-
localized fable, a substantial solidity. As Keats remarked,
Milton has the habit of "stationing" figures in relation to
solid objects: Satan and the Son look out on chaos from
the gates of hell and heaven; soaring birds "With clang
despised the ground, under a cloud In prospect."

One factor in such substantiality is explicit allusion
and simile, which link the nonhuman story with the
world—the fallen world—of geography and history and
experience. Even allusions to classical myth, mainly familiar, at once actualize and heighten the remote, ideal,
and preternatural. Although, in a sacred context, Milton
often labels these as pagan fictions, they elicit all his
imaginative and artistic power. In the fall of Mulciber
(I.738 f.) Homeric comedy is transmuted into romantic
sublimity by the poet's sense of space and of the contrast
between the diabolic figure and the pure serenity of
nature, and by the changes in rhythm from smooth float-
ing to the apparent sudden rush as the body nears earth
and then comes to rest:

> . . . and how he fell
> From heav'n, they fabled, thrown by angry Jove
> Sheer o'er the crystal battlements: from morn
> To noon he fell, from noon to dewy eve,
> A summer's day; and with the setting sun
> Dropped from the zenith like a falling star
> On Lemnos th' Aegean isle. Thus they relate,
> Erring. . . .

But, while myth supplies one kind of simile, Milton's similes draw upon the most heterogeneous materials and contribute much to both the actuality of the narrative and our imaginative realization and understanding of its import. Even when the core is traditional, he may add concrete particulars: Satan's shield is not merely like the moon but like the spotty globe seen through the telescope of Galileo in Fiesole. No simile was more traditional than the likening of an army to fallen leaves, but Satan's legions lay entranced

> Thick as autumnal leaves that strow the brooks
> In Vallombrosa, where th' Etrurian shades
> High overarched embower.

The name is concrete, melodious, and, in the juxtaposition of "shady valley" and a lake of fire, ironic. That simile suggests great numbers of prostrate angels, "Their glory withered" (to quote a later phrase). The ensuing and much more elaborate comparison with Pharaoh's host overwhelmed in the Red Sea adds both multitudinous motion and confusion of bodies and minds and an example of the fate of God's enemies. However important the descriptive function of similes—and in general of allusions, images, and epithets—they also carry the emotional charge of a moral or religious judgment. And the solid and literal continually merge with the metaphorical and symbolic: hell, chaos, heaven, and Eden are

all both material scenes and spiritual states. Visual
images abound, especially of motion, and Milton's other
senses are likewise active, directly or in metaphor. We
have observed how stirring his poetry of ideas can be
(though indeed all his poetry is that), and for another
example there are those lines (V.620 f.) that illustrate
his Platonic sense of the planetary orbits as a paradigm
of divine order: the dance of angels about the sacred
hill is a

> Mystical dance, which yonder starry sphere
> Of planets and of fixed in all her wheels
> Resembles nearest, mazes intricate,
> Eccentric, intervolved, yet regular
> Then most, when most irregular they seem;
> And in their motions harmony divine
> So smooths her charming tones that God's own ear
> Listens delighted.

This is Sir Thomas Browne's "mystical mathematics of
the city of heaven."

Any long poem, at least until recent times, demanded
stylization, and Renaissance theory and practice, looking
back to the highly stylized Virgil and Homer, to some
degree codified devices for achieving epic magnificence.
For Milton the poetry of Della Casa and Tasso and
Tasso's critical discourses were probably of special value.
But, even if the Italians had never existed, Milton's classical instincts and his conception of the religious and
prophetic function of poetry would have led him toward
Roman, Greek, and Hebraic grandeur. In composing
Paradise Lost he was not merely "a poet soaring in the
high region of his fancies with his garland and singing
robes about him." His epic style must be "answerable"
to his divine subject; it must raise the mind above mundane concerns to contemplation of first and last things.
Although "sublimity" has dropped out of the modern
critical lexicon, no other word is adequate. In Dr. John-

son's phrase, Milton's "natural port is gigantick loftiness." Almost everything said so far has had to do with Miltonic sublimity, but a little must be, and only a little can be, said about matters of style; proper discussion would need another book.

Elements of the grand style had appeared in Milton's earlier poems, especially the sonnets, and in the roughness and toughness of language, syntax, and image in the soaring or snorting prose, English and Latin. Under diction go unusual, exalted, and arresting words, coinages, words used in new meanings, punning plays on words, the shifting of parts of speech (adjectives as adverbs and nouns—"the vast abrupt"), the use of Latin derivatives in their literal sense ("error" for "wandering"). Then there are condensed and elliptical syntax, at once fluid and muscular; the placing of words and phrases for emphasis rather than in the order of prose; periodic sentences (like those that open books one and two); periphrases (which, like similes, do not merely elevate the fact but assess its significance). These and other devices—some of which had been used by Spenser, Sylvester, and George Sandys in his translation of Ovid—compel attention, heighten dignity, energy, and intensity, and govern imaginative and emotional responses. Milton's unique power in the exploitation of them has led to the common charge that he made English a foreign language. Yet to discount the charge one has only to open the poem almost anywhere and read; and close reading will show that the epic devices are richly functional and hardly ever mechanical. For all the bold and cunning pressures Milton exerts upon language, in its total effect his style is one of grand simplicity; it is only after rapidly assimilating the large cinematic impressions that we study the subtle details.

The placing of words and phrases with the freedom of an inflected language—something already practiced in

Milton's prose—yields continual advantages in expressive
emphasis:

> Him the Almighty Power
> Hurled headlong flaming from th' ethereal sky
> With hideous ruin and combustion down
> To bottomless perdition, there to dwell
> In adamantine chains and penal fire,
> Who durst defy th' Omnipotent to arms.

Recast in the order of prose (and bereft of rhythm), this
would be flat and limp. The force of the initial and
alliterative "Him" and "Hurled headlong" (Milton is
fond of a monosyllabic verb as the first word in a line)
carries on until, as a critic has said, Satan hits bottom,
where he is held by the regularity of "there . . . fire," and
the last line is the stronger for being delayed five lines
beyond its antecedent; the stock epithets, like Homer's,
recall accepted facts and free the imagination to receive
the central impact. The explosive but ordered finality of
that passage may be contrasted with the disorderly violence of evil energy, expressed partly by word order,
partly by the jostling of many verbs, in the lines where
Sin and Death, in parody of God's creativity, begin to
build their bridge to the world (X.282 f.):

> Then both from out hell gates into the waste
> Wide anarchy of Chaos damp and dark
> Flew diverse, and with power (their power was great)
> Hovering upon the waters; what they met
> Solid or slimy, as in raging sea
> Tossed up and down, together crowded drove
> From each side shoaling towards the mouth of hell.

Yet within the necessary stylization there is infinite
variety of diction and tone (including the serious use of
the comic or grotesque), and one pervasive thread is
quiet and direct simplicity, from "Brought death into the
world, and all our woe" or "There rest, if any rest can

harbor there" (the rhetorical pattern, *a:b:b:a,* though potent, is hardly noticed) to the last lines of the poem which were quoted above. In sublime simplicity nothing could surpass the invocation to Light. After the opening phrase, "Hail, holy Light," which sets the tone as religious, not scientific, the first few lines of theological speculation are technical and latinate, but the rest are in another vein. The change of scene from hell to heaven recalls—as we observed on an early page—the journeys of Orpheus and Aeneas to and up from the underworld, the blind poet's continuing love of the classics and above them of the Bible, his place in the line of blind prophet-poets, his visual darkness and his inner light:

> Yet not the more
> Cease I to wander where the Muses haunt
> Clear spring, or shady grove, or sunny hill,
> Smit with the love of sacred song; but chief
> Thee, Sion, and the flow'ry brooks beneath
> That wash thy hallowed feet, and warbling flow,
> Nightly I visit; nor sometimes forget
> Those other two equaled with me in fate,
> So were I equaled with them in renown,
> Blind Thamyris and blind Maeonides,
> And Tiresias and Phineus prophets old:
> Then feed on thoughts that voluntary move
> Harmonious numbers, as the wakeful bird
> Sings darkling, and in shadiest covert hid
> Tunes her nocturnal note. Thus with the year
> Seasons return; but not to me returns
> Day, or the sweet approach of ev'n or morn,
> Or sight of vernal bloom, or summer's rose,
> Or flocks, or herds, or human face divine;
> But cloud instead, and ever-during dark
> Surrounds me, from the cheerful ways of men
> Cut off, and for the book of knowledge fair
> Presented with a universal blank
> Of Nature's works to me expunged and razed,

And wisdom at one entrance quite shut out.
So much the rather thou, celestial Light,
Shine inward, and the mind through all her powers
Irradiate, there plant eyes, all mist from thence
Purge and disperse, that I may see and tell
Of things invisible to mortal sight.

If we want to know what "classical" writing is, this is
it. One general impression is of Milton's feeling of nor-
mality, of community with mankind; there is no trace of
sentimental softness, nothing of the self-pity and sense
of uniqueness found in some poems of the romantic age.
In keeping with that is the depersonalizing and general-
izing of both personal emotions and their objects. In the
first lines Milton records his unabated love of classical
poetry, though he sets it below the Bible; while the lines
are, as always, self-sufficient, they work a beautiful varia-
tion on the passage (*Georgics* II.475 f.) in which Virgil
declares his love of the Muses—*ingenti percussus amore*—
and his delight in the country even if he cannot attain to
higher cosmic themes. Milton gives a "prosaic" list (in
ascending order) of the everyday things of nature and
life from which a blind poet is cut off. Such an atmosphere has been created that the mere naming of the items
is—along with the rhythm—enough; and the list ends
with a quietly paradoxical phrase, the first adjective sug-
gesting the association of "friend with friend," the second
the creation of man in God's image and the miracle of
the human face. No less "prosaic," apart from the strongly
charged Miltonic "turn" (a phrase repeated in slightly
altered form), are the personal lines quoted above in the
second paragraph of this section. And neither passage
exhibits the predominantly Latin diction and syntax that
supposedly make the grand style a stiff brocade; indeed
many impressionistic judgments on this point, in regard
to the whole poem, are simply not in accord with the

facts. In any case, however bold or complicated Milton's syntax at times may be, his meaning is scarcely ever in doubt—as it often is in Shakespeare, though Shakespeare is always taken to represent the true genius of English.

As Milton said in his short and vigorous preface (which may reflect the recent debate on rhyme between Dryden and Sir Robert Howard), the use of blank verse for a heroic poem was a great innovation, and in using it he created a new world of expressive sound. His rhythms are so much a part of his total effect, indeed of his very meaning, that he has to be read aloud; even a few remarks on his style could not avoid rhythm. But the subtleties of Milton's versification are as impossible to deal with briefly as the subtleties of his style, and only a little can be said about some main principles. The basic fact is that Milton's unit is the ten-syllable line; it is essential to think of it in that way and not as an iambic pentameter with many substitutions, an idea which suggests contrived mechanics rather than complete freedom and flexibility. In Milton's blank verse the ten syllables (often achieved through elision and slurring, as in excerpts quoted here) are commonly grouped in pairs, which are most often iambs; but that is as far as one can go toward a general rule. The lines contain any number of stresses from three to eight, and these may differ markedly in degree and in position. The caesura or natural pause in the line falls most often of course in the middle section but is continually varied, and it may come even after the first syllable (as, in the extract above from the invocation to Light, "Day" is poised so arrestingly); the weight of the caesura varies like its position. Although, for the reasons indicated, the infinite variety of stress and tempo cannot begin to be measured with the usual blunt instrument, marks for stressed and unstressed syllables, the familiar opening lines may be crudely charted:

Ŏf mán's / fírst dís / ŏbéd / ĭēnce, // aňd / thĕ frúit
Ŏf thát / fŏrbíd / dĕn trée, // whŏse mór / tăl táste
Bróught deáth / ĭntŏ / thĕ wórld, // aňd áll / oŭr wóe,
Wĭth lóss / ŏf Éd / ĕn, // tĭll / óne gréat /ĕr Mán
Rĕstóre / us, // aňd / rĕgaín / thĕ blíss / fŭl séat,
Síng, Héav'n / lў̆ Múse, // thăt ŏn / thĕ séc /rĕt tóp. . . .

Here only one line is a regular iambic, and its movement
carries an effect of irrevocable finality, an effect felt likewise in "and all our woe" (a phrase that becomes a
leitmotiv throughout the poem). In the first line and the
beginning of the third the grouping of strong stresses
accentuates the thematic ideas. In line four the feminine
caesura (one that comes after a weak syllable) heightens
the idea of something gone wrong, while the phrases
that follow are mostly in the rising rhythm of reassurance. Readers might differ in stressing or not stressing
such words as "till," "us," and "that," in the last three
lines. In general, we read the weighted words slowly and
slide quickly over the rest.

This opening sentence has sixteen lines, a sufficient
example of what Milton in his preface refers to as "the
sense variously drawn out from one verse into another."
We observed how the use of run-on lines and strong
medial pauses (with some wrenching of normal word
order) gave the sonnets the character of blank-verse
paragraphs, and in the epic Milton had full scope for his
planetary wheelings. While the ten-syllable line (with its
endless internal variations) remains in our ear as a norm,
there is another system comprising the irregular rhythmic
units that flow from one caesura to another, so that we
have the combined pleasures of recurrence and surprise
manipulated by a supreme artist; and all these effects
contribute immeasurably to the sense of what is being
said. The continual changes of pace and stress operate
within "the enormous onward pressure of the great

stream on which you are embarked." In general Milton
compels a reading much more rapid than most blank
verse allows. As Mr. Eliot, a master of expressive rhythm,
has said, Milton's verse is never monotonous; its strength
and intricate refinements every reader must experience
for himself.

In the world of Hobbes and Newton and the Royal
Society, of travesties of the classical epics and *Hudibras*
and *The Country Wife, Paradise Lost* was an anachronism when it was published (although, as we shall see,
its fame soon mounted). But the science and skepticism
of the Augustan Enlightenment have now only historical
interest and *Paradise Lost* remains, an anachronism still.
No long poem in the world is maintained throughout at
concert pitch, not even the *Iliad* or *Odyssey* or *Aeneid*
and certainly not the *Divine Comedy*, which is often used
as a stick to beat Milton with. In its texture and structure, in all its imaginative variety and power, *Paradise
Lost* is an inexhaustible source of aesthetic pleasure of a
kind unique in English poetry. And, whatever theological
elements some readers may choose to ignore, the essential myth, the picture of the grandeur and misery of man,
remains "true," and infinitely more noble and beautiful
than anything modern literature has been able to provide.
The question is not how far the poem is worthy of our
attention, but how far we can make ourselves worthy
of it.

3

Paradise Regained

IN 1671 (or possibly 1670) *Paradise Regained* and *Samson Agonistes* were printed in one volume. When at Chalfont St. Giles, in the late summer of 1665, Thomas Ellwood returned the manuscript of *Paradise Lost* to Milton, they talked awhile about the poem and then, Ellwood reports,

I pleasantly said to him, "Thou hast said much here of *Paradise Lost*; but what hast thou to say of *Paradise Found?*" He made me no answer, but sat some time in a muse; then brake off that discourse and fell upon another subject.

Later, Ellwood added, Milton showed him *Paradise Regained*, saying that his young friend had put into his head a theme he had not thought of. Whatever is to be made of the honest but simple-minded Ellwood's account, the theme of *Paradise Regained* had been at least implicit in *Paradise Lost*. In the prelude to book nine, Milton had contrasted martial epic and romance with

> the better fortitude
> Of patience and heroic martyrdom
> Unsung;

and that poem had ended with Adam's comprehending the true way of life but without his being tested in practice. As the opening lines of *Paradise Regained* remind us, the story of Adam's fall invited a sequel on the second Adam, whose "firm obedience fully tried" raised a new Eden of the soul in the waste wilderness.

The title alone might suggest the crucifixion. Milton's choice of the encounter with Satan would be dictated not merely by reluctance to touch the gospels' unapproachable narratives but by several positive reasons: his predominant concern with religious and moral integrity confronted by temptation; the Renaissance tradition of the ideal hero—like Spenser's Guyon, whom Milton had cited in *Areopagitica*—as a potent example for ordinary men; the conception of this episode as a trial preliminary to Christ's final one; and, for a sequel to *Paradise Lost*, the logic of Satan's being defeated by a stronger antagonist than Adam. For all these purposes there would be support in Milton's theological view of the Son as subordinate to the Father, most conspicuously in the half-human role of Christ uncertain of his way at the beginning of his earthly mission. In regard to the form and scope of the poem, two general remarks of Milton's supply hints. As far back as the personal passage in the *Reason of Church Government*, in his survey of poetic genres, he had mentioned the book of Job as "a brief model" for an epic, and Job was evidently much in his mind in the composition of *Paradise Regained* (and of *Samson* also). And in the *Second Defence* Milton had spoken of the epic poet's describing, not the whole life of a hero, but one particular action.

Disparagement, or lukewarm commendation, of *Paradise Regained* began in Milton's lifetime. According to Phillips, it was generally considered

much inferior to the other, though he [Milton] could not hear with patience any such thing when related to him. Possibly the subject may not afford such variety of invention; but it is thought by the most judicious to be little or nothing inferior to the other for style and decorum.

The conventional charges have been chiefly that the poem lacks the splendors of *Paradise Lost*, that Christ is a cold embodiment of half-Stoic reason, that, since he is perfect virtue, there is no real conflict and drama, and that the total result is didactic dullness. While inveterate prejudice of any kind can seldom be eradicated, such complaints may be thought ill-founded; and of late years a number of notable critics have in various ways shown the real power of the poem. It is not Milton's fault if we do not share his moral passion, and the poem is cold only to the cold. As modern literature amply proves, we no longer respond to the Renaissance conception of the ideal hero, least of all to an exemplar of religious humility and righteousness.

Milton was not failing in a minor effort to carry on the mode of *Paradise Lost*; he was composing a quite different kind of poem. Everything is on a much smaller scale; and, though there is a little epic machinery (the councils in hell and heaven), the poem is virtually a dramatic debate with elaborate stage directions. The style, except for special reasons in a few passages, is deliberately plain, almost on the level of the gospels, and there is a corresponding simplicity of syntax and rhythm. The two principal characters are conceived in mainly human terms. For all his supernatural powers and momentary flashes of his old dignity and eloquence, Satan is a much diminished shadow of the "Archangel ruined," in the main a wily exponent of the world's values. One element of drama and suspense is furnished by Satan's urgent motive in his tempting of Christ: the being whose baptism has just received heavenly sanction is probably the agent destined by God to accomplish his destruction, and Satan must either confirm or remove the fear that has so long hung over him. And notwithstanding the stock criticism that we know Christ cannot waver or fall, a complementary element of drama is centered in him. His soliloquy (I.196 f.) shows his general understanding of his mission and eventual fate, yet he is in his human character not fully certain of his course of action or even of his own identity, and he must proceed step by step as God directs him; humble faith and obedience are the distinctive virtues of the second Adam. Also, if we think of Milton's public experience we feel an added pressure in the dramatic rejecting of all political action and the exalting of individual, inward strength, "heroic knowledge."

For his central pattern Milton followed Luke (4:1–13), where the temptation of the pinnacle came last, rather than Matthew (4:1–11), though he wove in much other material, biblical and historical. Satan appears after Christ has had his forty days of fasting and meditation in the wilderness. The first temptation, the demand that Christ, if he is the son of God, should turn the stones into bread, is summarily refused, for the reason given by Protestant theologians—that the performance of such a miracle would imply distrust of God's providence. Satan, whose disguise Christ has readily penetrated, declares that he admires virtue and has helped mankind through oracles and portents, and Christ vigorously contrasts the delusive oracles of history with his own role as God's living oracle, sent into the world to teach his will and to establish an inward oracle in pious hearts.

The second book opens with the bewildered dismay of the fishermen disciples whose master has so long been mysteriously absent. Their laments have the effect of isolating Christ even from his devoted followers, since they have expected him to free Israel from the Roman yoke and found an earthly kingdom. A similar note, though less overt, is heard in the troubled reflections of Mary. Christ's unworldly purity is suggested in another way by Belial's proposal, in an infernal council, to "Set

women in his eye and in his walk." Meanwhile Christ
feels hunger and dreams, not of feasts, but of the simple
food the ravens brought to Elijah. Satan returns and
presents a luxurious banquet, served by handsome youths
and nymphs

> And ladies of th' Hesperides, that seemed
> Fairer than feigned of old, or fabled since
> Of fairy damsels met in forest wide
> By knights of Logres, or of Lyonnesse,
> Lancelot or Pelleas, or Pellenore.

These chiming syllables are (along with III.338 f.)
Milton's last testimony to his youthful love of romance.
Charles Lamb, in "Grace before Meat," found this banquet needlessly opulent; but it tells us of Satan's scale of
values and of the gulf between him and his adversary.

The first temptation, the changing of stones into bread,
and the third (the pinnacle) involve Christ's supposed
divinity; the second moves from the rational to the religious level. The banquet is the first of the half-dozen
ascending stages into which Milton divides the second
temptation, that of "the kingdoms of the world." All of
Satan's subsequent offers are based on his belief that
Christ is aiming at an earthly throne, and Christ rejects
the world's prizes with a temperance and magnanimity
both pagan and Christian. After the appeal to the senses
comes wealth, which Christ puts aside with a Renaissance humanist's fervent eulogy of the true king who
rules his own "Passions, desires, and fears." Glory, the
praise of "A miscellaneous rabble" (a view of the popu-
lace more classical and Miltonic—and Shakespearian—
than Christlike), is set against God's approval of the
righteous man, the kind of true fame that had been celebrated in *Lycidas*. And, in contrast with the false glory
of conquering heroes, there is Socrates, who, next after
Job (and, we think, next after Christ),

By what he taught and suffered for so doing,
For truth's sake suffering death unjust, lives now
Equal in fame to proudest conquerors.

Satan now makes a nobler proposal which is the more insidious because it had once presented itself to Christ's own mind (a parallel object had animated Milton)—the patriotic deliverance of Israel from Rome. In Christ's refusal the religious motive transcends the classical and rational; he stands on obedient trust in God's providence and direction. Satan then arrives at the specific temptation of the kingdoms of the world. From a mountaintop he shows Christ the whole East; little Judea, between the empires of Parthia and Rome, cannot survive without the aid of one or the other, and Satan advises Parthia. Christ will have nothing to do with power politics. Increasingly disturbed by his failures, Satan exhibits the western panorama of Rome, the city itself and the empire stretching from Britain to the

utmost Indian isle Taprobanè,
Dusk faces with white silken turbants wreathed.

Here above all Christ is placed firmly in his historical setting, and Milton condenses the familiar learning of a lifetime in a picture which, though short, includes every major item that we associate with the "Queen of the Earth." Satan goes on to urge more than the freeing of Judea: since the aged Tiberius is given up to vice, Christ may well seize even the imperial throne. But Christ asserts the Miltonic conviction that a corrupt people cannot be made free; when his season comes, it

shall to pieces dash
All monarchies besides throughout the world,
And of my kingdom there shall be no end.

Satan now adds to the temptation of the kingdoms a final piece of advice that appears to be original with

Milton—to learn the rich wisdom of Greece, which a great emperor must possess if he is to hold his own with Gentiles. There follows a picture which is another distillation of a lifetime's devotion (and which telescopes Greek history and presents it as if it were, like Rome, contemporary):

> Athens, the eye of Greece, mother of arts
> And eloquence, native to famous wits
> Or hospitable, in her sweet recess,
> City or suburban, studious walks and shades;
> See there the olive grove of Academe,
> Plato's retirement, where the Attic bird
> Trills her thick-warbled notes the summer long;
> There flow'ry hill Hymettus with the sound
> Of bees' industrious murmur oft invites
> To studious musing; there Ilissus rolls
> His whispering stream. . . .

Satan runs over the poets of lyric, epic, and tragedy, the orators,

> whose resistless eloquence
> Wielded at will that fierce democraty;

and the philosophers from Socrates to the Stoics. All these

> will render thee a king complete
> Within thyself, much more with empire joined.

These last lines—apart from the last phrase—recall Christ's own earlier definition of a true king.

Christ replies that, whether or not he knows these things,

> He who receives
> Light from above, from the Fountain of Light,
> No other doctrine needs, though granted true;
> But these are false, or little else but dreams,
> Conjectures, fancies, built on nothing firm.

Socrates, the wisest of all, professed "To know this only, that he nothing knew"; Plato "to fabling fell and smooth conceits"; the Stoics especially confused philosophic pride with virtue. The philosophers, ignorant of themselves and of God, of creation and man's fall, talk much of the soul,

> but all awry,
> And in themselves seek virtue, and to themselves
> All glory arrogate, to God give none.

(As Christ goes on, Milton's classical instincts betray themselves, in lines 318–321, in a veiled allusion to the myth of Ixion.) A man may be "Deep versed in books and shallow in himself," "As children gathering pebbles on the shore." Greek poems celebrating false gods, with "swelling epithets, thick laid As varnish on a harlot's cheek," cannot be compared

> With Sion's songs, to all true tastes excelling,
> Where God is praised aright, and godlike men,
> The Holiest of Holies, and his saints;
> Such are from God inspired, not such from thee;
> Unless where moral virtue is expressed
> By light of nature not in all quite lost.

This whole exchange has shocked and pained many readers. Satan's eulogy of Athens, we feel sure, came from Milton's heart; did Christ's repudiation of Greek culture come from the same heart? Is the aged Puritan turning and rending the literature and thought that had done so much to make him an artist and a lover of virtue and liberty? But second thoughts should remove the grounds for dismay. The gist of the matter is that, if there must be a showdown between the light of nature, which may nourish irreligious pride, and the light of Christian truth, on which man's earthly and eternal welfare depend, the choice is clear. Milton had always ranked the Bible far above the classics—in the *Reason of*

Church Government (where he had stressed its literary art), in the *Apology for Smectymnuus* and *Of Education*, and in the invocations of *Paradise Lost*. While we do not share his conception of the Bible (and even he gave still higher authority to inward guidance), we can hardly deny, whatever our classical devotion, that the biblical vision of good and evil touches levels beyond that of the classics.

All Christian humanists, with all their reverence for ancient wisdom, made Milton's fundamental distinction, and, for him as for them, the hierarchy of values was so completely accepted that no active inner conflict was involved. We might remember Milton's old antagonist, Bishop Hall, whose assimilation of Seneca's moral wisdom and style had won him the title of "our English Seneca." In *Heaven upon Earth* (1606) Hall said what Milton would have largely endorsed:

Never any heathen wrote more divinely; never any philosopher more probably. Neither would I ever desire better master, if to this purpose I needed no other mistress than nature. But this in truth is a task which nature hath never without presumption undertaken, and never performed without imperfection. . . . And if she could have truly effected it alone, I know not what employment in this life she should have left for grace to busy herself about, nor what privilege it should have been here below to be a Christian, since this that we seek is the noblest work of the soul, and in which alone consists the only heaven of this world; this is the sum of all human desires: which when we have attained, then only we begin to live, and are sure we cannot thenceforth live miserably. No marvel then if all the heathen have diligently sought after it, many wrote of it, none attained it. Not Athens must teach this lesson, but Jerusalem.

Though Milton never ceased to cherish reason, in his disillusioned old age he came more and more to value humble faith and practice. Some of the lines quoted from

Paradise Regained remind us of the fallen angels in hell, who

> reasoned high
> Of providence, foreknowledge, will, and fate,
> Fixed fate, free will, foreknowledge absolute,
> And found no end, in wand'ring mazes lost.

We are reminded too of the discourses on astronomy in book eight, of the danger of being led astray by speculation on things remote from use and from the chief ends of life. The learned Milton had his share of his century's religious fear of "curiosity," of intemperance in the quest of knowledge. And this strain was not merely English or Puritan; it appeared in some continental writers of the Renaissance and in such men as Donne and Fulke Greville.

Finally, some considerations grow directly out of the context. Things good in themselves may be tainted by their source or the motives that attend them; Greek culture is put by Satan on a par with biblical truth and urged as an aid to political power. Then dramatic decorum, and perhaps Milton's long practice in debate, require that Christ, being what he is, should make a more unqualified judgment than Milton himself would. For Milton, to be sure, it is absolute, but it is also relative. Classical wisdom is good so far as it goes: Christ's earlier exaltation of Socrates as a true hero, his account of a true king, and his general repudiation of worldly glory are, as we observed, in accord with Renaissance humanism. And this same volume, we remember, contained a drama modeled on the works of Aeschylus, Sophocles, and Euripides, "the three tragic poets unequaled yet by any, and the best rule to all who endeavor to write tragedy." We cannot doubt that both the eulogy of Athens and the higher eulogy of Sion came from the poet's heart.

To return to the text, the baffled Satan reveals his own

nature and Christ's in a query that carries unconscious as
well as conscious irony:

> Since neither wealth, nor honor, arms nor arts,
> Kingdom nor empire pleases thee, nor aught
> By me proposed in life contemplative,
> Or active, tended on by glory, or fame,
> What dost thou in this world?

The second temptation ended, our sense of Christ's isola-
tion is heightened by his being left alone to face a new
kind of hostile pressure, a night of storm and howling
ghosts and furies conjured up by Satan. If Christ has
hitherto seemed secure and invulnerable, he is pictured
now with reverent compassion:

> Ill wast thou shrouded then,
> O patient Son of God, yet only stood'st
> Unshaken. . . .

> . . . .
> while thou
> Sat'st unappalled in calm and sinless peace.

In the morning Satan returns, more sure that he is con-
fronting his "fatal enemy," although so far Christ has
shown himself "To the utmost of mere man both wise and
good, Not more." The third temptation, handled swiftly,
is a challenge to Christ to prove his divinity—or his presumption—by standing on the pinnacle of the temple of
Jerusalem:

> To whom thus Jesus: "Also it is written,
> 'Tempt not the Lord thy God.'" He said, and stood.
> But Satan smitten with amazement fell,
> As when Earth's son Antaeus. . . .

> . . . .

> So after many a foil the Tempter proud,
> Renewing fresh assaults, amidst his pride
> Fell whence he stood to see his victor fall.

To quote the succinct comment of Arthur Woodhouse:

It is easy to miss the full drama and the irony concentrated in these few lines. Satan's intention is that Christ shall fall and the result will answer his question. His injunction to stand is purely ironical: that it is possible, he never for a moment conceives. But if Satan can be ironical, so can Christ and the event. For the first and only time, he complies with Satan's suggestion; but it is not in surrender to Satan: it is in obedience to God—like Samson's going to the festival of Dagon. This is Christ's supreme act of obedience and trust, and it is also the long-awaited demonstration of divinity. The poem's two themes are finally and securely united; and "Tempt not the Lord thy God" carries a double meaning, for, in addition to its immediate application, it is Christ's first claim to participate in the Godhead. In an instant, and by the same event, Satan receives his answer and Christ achieves full knowledge of himself.*

Christ is carried down to a flowery valley by angels who bring him food and hymn his divine nature and achievement, the founding of a fairer paradise for Adam's sons. The short and quiet ending at once sustains that theme and restores the great exemplar to his humble setting:

> Thus they the Son of God, our Saviour meek,
> Sung Victor, and from heavenly feast refreshed
> Brought on his way with joy; he unobserved
> Home to his mother's house private returned.

* "Theme and Pattern in *Paradise Regained*," *University of Toronto Quarterly*, 25 (1955–1956), 181. This interpretation of Christ's words, it may be said, accords with one of the less favored theological traditions inherited by the seventeenth century and is not accepted by some modern critics of Milton. They see in Milton the more orthodox idea that Christ is rejecting a gratuitous and presumptuous appeal to God's power. But this view may be thought to greatly lessen the dramatic force of the incident, which Milton seems to take as the climactic and special revelation of Christ's divinity.

4

Samson Agonistes

Samson Agonistes may have been composed at any time during 1660–1670, but, since Paradise Lost was apparently not finished until 1663–1665, it seems unlikely that Milton would have interrupted the epic to write the drama, and unlikely also that he would not have followed up the epic with its sequel. We may then—if we are quite unmoved by recent arguments for a date before 1660— think of Samson as his last poetic utterance. For some readers it is the most completely satisfying of the later works. While it has not the vast scope, complexity, variety, and splendor of Paradise Lost, it presents no theological barriers; and, in contrast with Paradise Regained, its hero (though in theological tradition one of the prototypes of Christ) is a wholly human sinner who attains spiritual regeneration only after touching the depths of misery and despair.

Milton was experimental to the last, and Samson was a bold novelty in form and style. The blank verse, obviously remote from the sweeping periods of Paradise Lost, has a colloquial irregularity more massive, rugged, and sinewy than the "prosaic" plainness of Paradise Regained. The texture, it has been truly said, gives the Greekless reader a more authentic sense of the style of Greek tragedy than any translation of an actual play. This general character and tone are heightened by Milton's use, in choric odes and some speeches, of more or less short lines which have a special expressive value in following closely the movement of thought and feeling. These short lines are not free verse of the modern kind; they can be scanned as irregular combinations of regular metrical feet, although Milton doubtless composed them in accordance with the free syllabic principles that governed his verse, and they are commonly parts of larger rhythmical and syntactic units. Some effects are illustrated in lines 80–82 of Samson's first speech:

Ó dárk, / dárk, dárk, // ămíd / thĕ bláze / ŏf nóon,
Ĭrrĕcóv / ĕráb / lў dárk, // tótăl / ĕclípse,
Wĭthóut / áll hópe / ŏf dáy.

The first four syllables, all long, depict Samson's condition, in contrast with the three following iambs that depict the bright world about him. In the second line the rising—one might say struggling—rhythm of the first half (an anapest and two iambs) shifts to a trochee in "total"; and the juxtaposition of two stressed syllables at the caesura explosively shatters the rhythm and intensifies the emotion. The third line links itself in sense and rhythm to the second half of the first, but with the negation that belongs to Samson's darkness. Other effects appear in 631–635:

Thĕnce fáint / ĭngs, // swóon / ĭngs ŏf / dĕspáir,
Ănd sénse / ŏf Héav'n's / dĕsér / tĭon.
    Í wás / hĭs núrs / lĭng ónce // ănd chóice /dĕlíght,
Hĭs dés / tĭned frŏm / thĕ wómb,
Prómĭsed/bў héaven/lў més/săge//twíce/dĕscénd/ĭng.

Here the smooth flow and strong endings of the third and fourth lines sustain the idea of Samson's former glory and assurance; in the other lines feminine caesuras and feminine line-endings suggest failure and loss.

Whatever Milton's early admiration for Shakespeare, he himself was not writing for the stage, and we should expect such a scholarly poet to follow the Greeks (and, as he notes in his preface, the Italians). The drama reminds us in various ways of all three of the Greek tragic poets. The epic simplicity of form, the predominance of the protagonist, and the author's passionate concern with righteousness may be called Aeschylean. The repeated testing of the protagonist's will and integrity, the pervasive irony, and the function of the chorus recall Sophocles. The strain of intellectualism and the self-defensive prominence given to a "bad" woman suggest Euripides. But of course Milton did not deliberately aim at such a combination of qualities; he had not only a life-long saturation in Greek tragedy but temperamental and artistic affinities with its authors, so that, as usual, he could work with entire ease and freedom within a convention. *Samson* is the one tragedy in English that can stand beside the ancient originals. Two plays which are relatively close to it—though not very close—are *Prometheus Bound* and *Oedipus at Colonus*.

Beginning, like the Greeks, on the eve of the catastrophe, Milton brings in other events of Samson's career by way of retrospective allusion. The brawny warrior of the book of Judges, the Heracles of Hebrew story, is endowed with a heroic character and a Hebraic conscience. As the drama opens, on the festival of Dagon, the Philistine god, the blind captive is led out of prison for a breath of fresh air. His long speech describes the pains of blindness and captivity, his utter debasement, his bitter sense of God's desertion:

> Ask for this great deliverer now, and find him
> Eyeless in Gaza at the mill with slaves. . . .

But although the bulk of Samson's speech is self-centered, a few lines near the middle of it contain the seed of ultimate recovery, an acknowledgement of his own responsibility for his lot. As the drama develops, self-pity and wounded pride and reproaches of God give way by degrees to clear-eyed and humble recognition of his sins and deserved sufferings.

In the large ironic pattern, each of the first four "acts" brings about a result contrary to that expected by the interlocutor. The chorus, though sympathetic, are "Job's comforters" and they turn the knife in Samson's wound by questioning his marriages with Philistine women. He is roused to the defense "That what I motioned was of God"; moreover, if the Israelites are still in subjection, it is because they failed to follow up his successes. (We meet here that recurrent Miltonic conviction, which usually seems to be topical as well as historical, that nations grown corrupt fall readily into bondage.) Samson's well-meaning but unimaginative father likewise rouses Samson to opposition, but on a higher level: Manoa's blaming of God elicits Samson's full confession of his own guilt and a declaration that his present servitude is much less base than his former servitude to Dalila. Manoa also turns the knife in his son's wound by reminding him that he has brought contempt upon the God of Israel and glory to Dagon, a reproach that draws from his son a still more contrite confession, and with it the belief that God will yet assert himself and make Dagon stoop. Manoa's happy report of his negotiations with the Philistines for ransom further deepens Samson's misery. Indeed the upward movement—which, if wholly steady, might have come to seem contrived—now undergoes a prolonged reversal. Samson sinks into abject despair and longs only for death. And the choric ode is an arraignment of God's ways which goes far beyond Adam's and which, though it will be answered in the end, is unmitigated here.

An extravagant nautical image heralds the approach

of Dalila, who has all the finery and perfume and attendants she has gained with the proceeds of betrayal. Samson is stirred at once to vehement anger. Dalila's apologies and defenses are spiced with sensual invitation, but her "fair enchanted cup, and warbling charms" have no more power over him (this last of Milton's allusions to Circe takes us back to his first Latin Elegy). Her allurements failing, Dalila turns on Samson to rejoice in the enduring fame she has won as a heroine of her nation. His renewed strength and confidence are carried further in his colloquy with the Philistine giant Harapha, who comes to inspect the fallen champion. When Samson's contempt for Harapha's armor brings the charge of black art in his own martial feats, Samson replies: "My trust is in the living God . . . ," and he challenges Harapha to decide by combat between Israel's God and Dagon. A still stronger testimony of his state of mind is his next speech, a humble admission, to his scornful enemy, of his sins and just punishment, joined with the hope of God's pardon and a repeated challenge. Harapha goes off "in a sultry chafe," and Samson shows a quietly lucid understanding of Harapha's embarrassment and of the limits of affliction he can himself endure; if death is to be his fate,

> it may with mine
> Draw their own ruin who attempt the deed.

The chorus recall his former prowess, when he was

> With plain heroic magnitude of mind
> And celestial vigor armed,

but they assume that he can now be only a hero of patient suffering.

The cause of Samson's new confidence is made clearer when he refuses to go to the feast and entertain the Philistines. To the officer's warning, "Regard thyself, this

will offend them highly," he answers "Myself? my conscience and internal peace"; he has come far from "Myself
my sepulchre, a moving grave" (102). Even the chorus
urge him to obey, pointing out that he works daily for his
captors. He replies:

> Not in their idol-worship, but by labor
> Honest and lawful to deserve my food
> Of those who have me in their civil power.

The reply is of the same kind as that of Socrates to the
friends who wished to arrange his escape from prison
and death. One of the impressive and Miltonic things in
the latter part of the drama is that Samson's humble
repentance and faith in God's restored favor bring, not
emotionalism, but a quiet Socratic rationality, fortitude,
and fearlessness. When he changes his mind and goes,
because of "Some rousing motions in me," a recognition
of God's directing providence, he can assure the chorus
that he will incur no dishonor: "The last of me or no
I cannot warrant." In pronouncing a benediction the
chorus recall the angel who attended his birth, the divine
blessing Samson had recalled in his first despairing
speech.

The last act is the last irony. Manoa's good hopes of a
ransom, of nursing his son at home, give place to the
messenger's account of the feast and Samson's feats of
strength ("performed, as reason was, obeying") and his
prayerful approach to the final one. The choric lament
contrasts the *hubris* of the Philistines, upon whom God
sent "a spirit of frenzy" (akin to the Greek Ate or Furies),
with the inward illumination of the blind Samson, who
in a climactic image is likened to the phoenix, the age-old
Christian symbol of death and rebirth (though here
expressly used of earthly fame). Manoa sadly glorifies
his son in lines which may represent the last phase of
Milton's "classical" art:

> Nothing is here for tears, nothing to wail
> Or knock the breast, no weakness, no contempt,
> Dispraise, or blame, nothing but well and fair,
> And what may quiet us in a death so noble.

Manoa will raise a monument to be kept as a shrine—a contrast with the one that Dalila anticipates. But Manoa, and the chorus, see only the external fact, that God has unexpectedly returned

> And to his faithful champion hath in place
> Bore witness gloriously;

they have not comprehended the nature of Samson's inward struggle and victory.

The briefest outline indicates the larger ironies of the drama, and the texture is full of ironic ambiguities. "Agonistes" means more than an ordinary participant in public games; and Samson's opening line, "A little onward lend thy guiding hand," is more than an injunction to his attendant. If Greek decorum is violated by the sense, especially in Samson, of an immediate relationship with God, the violation is hardly felt as such, in the main because Milton keeps ideas and beliefs strictly within the Hebraic frame. A few classical allusions—to Atlas (150), Stoic consolations against calamity (652–662), Circe (934–935)—are more or less veiled. What is much more important, no specifically Christian doctrines are admitted, no clear statement of the working of grace, not even faith in Samson's immortality (unless that is contained in Manoa's literal "Home to his father's house"); no flights of angels sing him to his rest. It has been said that a Christian with an assured belief in Providence cannot write a tragedy. But Milton was a Christian, and *Samson* is a tragedy; belief in Providence does not preclude what, in a limited human view, is tragic catastrophe. But one does not need any religious beliefs to be greatly moved by Milton's picture of pride, guilt, suffer-

ing, despair, and recovery; and the final vindication of
God's providential order does not, any more than in some
Greek plays, nullify the tragic sense of the mystery of
pain and evil.

It seems clear that in Samson Milton saw a partial
parallel to his own experience. One passage in the
chorus's indictment of God's justice (692 f.) must allude
to the Restoration government's treatment of the regicides, dead and living; and the lines go on to the "Painful
diseases and deformed" of premature old age, which
remind us of Milton's severe pangs of gout. In general,
of course, we think of the blind and defeated revolutionist in Restoration London as "Eyeless in Gaza at the
mill with slaves"; but parallels need not be stretched to
include Mary Powell and Milton's father ("I cannot
praise thy marriage choices, son"). Though the early
biographers do not suggest dormant fires under the quiet
routine of Milton's later life, the subject itself and the
excitement of composition could hardly fail to stir
thoughts of the revolution and its failure; and if we
remember his tracts of 1660, we may think that his chief
temptation, like Samson's, was despair. Such personal
involvement helps to explain the energy and intensity of
the drama. Yet it is not less significant that even in such
a work Milton preserved complete impersonality; there
is not a detail or sentiment that does not belong to the
story of Samson, and the poet's emotions, whatever they
may have been, were wholly sublimated. If Samson is in
some sense Milton, or an England which may rouse herself after sleep, that is an overtone; Milton's theme is the
grand theme of all his last works (as, in less dark days,
it had been of Comus and Lycidas), God's providence
sustaining and guiding individual righteousness or
regeneration.

═══════════════

5

Last Years and Writings and Early Fame

O F MILTON'S BIOGRAPHY only a little remains to be recorded. The *Poems* of 1645 had to wait until 1673 for a second edition. To the first collection, now slightly revised in places, Milton added his two earliest English poems, *On the Death of a Fair Infant* and *At a Vacation Exercise*, ten of the later sonnets, the Latin ode to John Rous, the two sets of Psalms translated in 1648 and 1653, some small items, and a reprint of the tract on education.

The revision of *Paradise Lost* and the composition of *Paradise Regained* and *Samson*, and the preparation for the press and proofreading of three volumes of poetry—the latter tasks being especially laborious since they required the poet's ears and amanuenses' eyes—might seem enough labor for Milton's last decade. But he also produced various works in prose, of which some had been more or less done at earlier times. Several of the books he turned out were of kinds that the smallest modern writer would hardly stoop to, but Milton's heart or mind "The lowliest duties on herself did lay"; he was still a Renaissance humanist. In 1669 and 1672 he published textbooks of simplified Latin grammar and logic. The *History of Britain,* which he had evidently given up any thought of finishing, was printed as a substantial fragment in 1670; the frontispiece was the Faithorne engraving of the author. In 1673, in the midst of renewed debate on the toleration of Nonconformity, Milton put forth his last tract, *Of True Religion, Heresy, Schism, Toleration: and what best means may be used against the growth of Popery*, a short and mild plea for truly scriptural Protestantism, with charitable tolerance for all except "the only or the greatest heresy." In the spring or summer of 1674 came a volume containing Milton's Latin letters to friends and his seven Cambridge prolusions, and, in this same summer, a few months before his death, the second edition of *Paradise Lost*.

To round out the record, some posthumous books may be added here. The account of the *History of Britain* in Part Three (5) noted the later publication of a deleted passage; it appeared in 1681 as *Mr. John Milton's Character of the Long Parliament and Assembly of Divines*. *A Brief History of Moscovia* (1682), which Milton had written before he lost his sight, amply confirms what many allusions in the epics suggest, his interest in voyages and travels and geography; the small book treated not only Russia but other eastward countries "as far as Cathay." The material was avowedly "gathered from the writings of several eye-witnesses"—in particular the collections of Hakluyt and Purchas—but it was skillfully selected, condensed, and reworked. Following in the tradition of the Étiennes, Milton had long labored on a Latin dictionary, and his notes were utilized by Edward Phillips and others in dictionaries published in 1684 and 1693. Phillips translated *Letters of State, Written by Mr. John Milton* (1694), with the prefatory life that has so often been quoted; in this book Phillips printed for the first time the sonnets to Fairfax and Cromwell and the second sonnet to Cyriack Skinner, and reprinted the sonnet to Vane which had appeared in George Sikes's book on Vane (1662). Collected editions of Milton's prose works were issued in 1697 and 1698; the latter was

Toland's. The large Latin treatise on Christian doctrine, which he evidently hoped might provide a firm scriptural basis for Protestantism, was not published until 1825; it was thought, said the anonymous biographer, who himself was broadly tolerant, that the work was not printed because of what modern scholars call Milton's heresies.

Milton died on or about November 9, 1674, a month short of his sixty-sixth birthday, and on the 12th he was buried beside his father in the chancel of St. Giles Cripplegate. The cause of death may have been heart failure due to hardening of the arteries; Aubrey's phrase was "the gout struck in." According to the anonymous biographer, "He died in a fit of the gout, but with so little pain or emotion that the time of his expiring was not perceived by those in the room"—a sentence which was mostly taken over by Anthony Wood and which Dr. Johnson condensed and elevated into "He died by a quiet and silent expiration" (and that passed into T. S. Eliot's "one who died blind and quiet"). The funeral, said Toland, was attended by "All his learned and great friends in London, not without a friendly concourse of the vulgar."

In a nuncupative will, recorded a few months before his death by his brother Christopher, the lawyer, Milton left his personal estate (of less than £1000) to his "loving wife." To "the unkind children" he had by his first wife he left her dowry of £1000, with arrears of interest since 1642; this dowry, which Richard Powell had never paid, the Powell family was now able to pay. The will was contested by the daughters, perhaps with the support of the Powells (Richard Powell's widow was still alive), and was disallowed in court. In the end Milton's widow kept £600 and paid £100 to each of the daughters. Although Deborah, the youngest, went along with her sisters in the suit, she had apparently been on better terms than they with their father and, as we observed,

retained affectionate memories; she married Abraham
Clarke, a Dublin weaver, in 1674 and died in England in
the same year as Mrs. Milton, 1727.

Within twenty-five years of Milton's death five biographies were written—which was unprecedented recognition for an English author and private citizen. The first
four of these, to be sure, were short. The identity of the
anonymous biographer—whose account was not printed—
has occasioned much discussion; perhaps the most likely
candidate is Milton's early pupil and later friend, Cyriack
Skinner. The notes of the infinitely curious and usually
careful John Aubrey have been printed a number of
times by modern editors; he sent them in 1681 to Anthony Wood, the Oxford antiquary. Wood's life, which
appeared in his *Fasti Oxonienses* (1691), was drawn
chiefly from the anonymous manuscript, Aubrey, and
Milton's books, and has no independent authority; apart
from a better list of Milton's writings, Wood added
almost nothing except some royalist rancor. Edward
Phillips's more ample life (1694) supplied a good deal
of new information. John Toland's long introduction to
his edition of the prose works (1698) was largely devoted
to expounding Milton's liberal ideas, but he drew upon
personal passages in the prose and added some new
items. Two later contributions were the pages in Thomas
Ellwood's autobiography (1714) on his relations with
Milton, and the big book on *Paradise Lost* (1734) by the
Jonathan Richardsons, father and son; the father—like
Toland—knew people who had known Milton, and was
able to make a few nice additions (and some good
critical comments).

From the start of his pamphleteering until his death
Milton was attacked, at length or in brief gibes, about
four times as often as he was cited with approval, and
the chorus of abuse was loudest in 1660. From that year
up through the revolution of 1689 to the end of the cen-

tury Milton's name recurred in debate, and his libertarian ideas, while still vilified by Tories, were increasingly praised and echoed. We have noted the collected editions of his prose in 1697 and 1698. We cannot follow either the acrimonious or the laudatory line, though we might observe that political antagonism had its last notable expression in Dr. Johnson's *Lives of the Poets* (1779) and that Milton had illustrious admirers in America.

As we have seen, most of Milton's many visitors wanted to talk with the publicist, not the poet, but in the last years of his life the poet was coming into his own. Some facts of the marketplace indicate the growing momentum with which *Paradise Lost* rose to unique eminence. The sale of the first thirteen hundred copies in about a year and a half was not bad, in a London and an age strongly devoted to satirical and licentious wit. Simmons brought out second and third editions in 1674 and 1678 and then sold his rights, which passed eventually to the reputable Jacob Tonson. Tonson's folio editions, the fourth, fifth, and sixth (1688, 1692, 1695), show mounting demand and prestige; the 1688 edition—which was illustrated— carried a list of over five hundred subscribers, a number of them from the aristocracy of rank and letters. The 1695 edition contained 321 pages of notes by a school- master, Patrick Hume; this edition—which in the same year was issued with the other poems as *The Poetical Works of Mr. John Milton*—was the first edition of an English poem annotated in the way the ancient classics had been.

The influence of Milton's early *Poems* seems to have first shown itself in a book (1647) by the plagiarizing poetaster, Robert Baron; in several apparent echoes in Marvell's *Flecknoe*, *Tom May's Death*, and *First Anni- versary*; in a great many echoes in Edward Benlowes's religious allegory, *Theophila* (1652); and in quotations in Joshua Poole's *English Parnassus: or, A Help to English*

Poesy (1657). Poetry, to be sure, was not a predominant concern in the years of the revolution and the Commonwealth, and of course there were no reviews and modern arts of publicity. This last fact bears also on the early reception of *Paradise Lost*. One cannot omit two famous anecdotes told by Richardson, although the data of both raise some questions. When Sir John Denham the poet one morning entered the House of Commons "with a sheet, wet from the press, in his hand," a fellow M.P. asked "What have you there, Sir John?" "Part of the noblest poem that ever was wrote in any language or in any age." Richardson also related—to use the note he made when he heard the tale rather than his printed version—that the Earl of Dorset, happening on the poem in a bookshop and reading a few lines, "bought it for a trifle, for it was then but waste paper," and, after reading it "many times over," sent it to Dryden; Dryden, who had not seen it before, returned it with the remark that this poet "had cut us all out."

Aubrey was the first narrator of a still more famous story about the origin of Dryden's operatic version of the poem, *The State of Innocence:*

John Dryden, Esq., Poet Laureate, who very much admires him, and went to him to have leave to put his *Paradise Lost* into a drama in rhyme. Mr. Milton received him civilly and told him he would give him leave to tag his verses.*

Milton's magnanimity can be appreciated by those who remember his preface to *Paradise Lost* and still more by those who remember *The State of Innocence* (though Dryden's study of Milton and Virgil apparently led him toward a more resonant couplet); when he published his work in 1677, Dryden handsomely acknowledged its great

---

* Richardson, in referring to the story, explained that "the fashion was in those days to wear much ribbon, which some adorned with tags of metal at the ends."

inferiority to its model. Tonson's 1688 edition of *Paradise Lost* had under Milton's portrait the epigram, "Three poets in three distant ages born," in which Dryden affirmed that Milton combined the powers of Homer and Virgil. In prose, writing as a sober Augustan critic, Dryden mixed eulogy with censure of flat stretches, blank verse, archaic diction, and other faults. To sum things up briefly, the fame of *Paradise Lost* was well established before the appearance of Addison's eighteen papers in the *Spectator* (1712), in which the criteria were the *Iliad* and *Aeneid* and neoclassical doctrines. Tributes of poetic imitation multiplied rapidly, in Thomson's *Seasons* (1726 f.) and a swarm of other works. Milton's influence became enormous, though he cannot be blamed for the common idea that Miltonic blank verse could be achieved by the avoiding of rhyme and the use of latinate diction. The fame and fate of the minor poems must here be passed by.

CONCLUSION

In the romantic age response to Milton—whose name meant chiefly *Paradise Lost*—took on a new and far richer vitality and moved along a new road, or rather along two divergent roads. On the one hand Milton was seen as the great rebel against authority and his Satan as a heroic projection of himself. Everyone knows Blake's saying: "The reason Milton wrote in fetters when he wrote of Angels and God, and at liberty when of Devils and Hell, is because he was a true Poet and of the Devil's party without knowing it." The main agents of this distortion, Blake and Shelley, made Milton over in their own revolutionary image, with small regard for his actual and earnest beliefs and convictions and the kind of rebellion these inspired. This "Satanist" misreading, which was not unnatural in such ardent rebels as its first proponents, persisted through the nineteenth century and into our own time, although it lost its original revolutionary impulse and dwindled into a conventional literary attitude.

Another view, which may be said to have had its representative beginnings in Hazlitt and Keats, was perhaps more common during the same long period and was more in keeping with ordinary nineteenth-century liberalism. This view slighted or dismissed Milton's religious and moral principles and purposes and concentrated on purely aesthetic appreciation of his imaginative power and beauties of texture and sound. (One distinguished

early exception was the religious and omniscient Coleridge, who belonged to neither of these two main lines of
opinion and who on some questions concerning *Paradise
Lost* anticipated the best modern criticism.) This aesthetic attitude, though it brought some new general and
local insights, was in its way almost as inadequate or
wrongheaded as "Satanism." It was crystallized in 1900
in Sir Walter Raleigh's notorious dictum that "The
Paradise Lost is not the less an eternal monument because it is a monument to dead ideas." The dictum is an
incidental reminder that—Coleridge again excepted—
nineteenth-century critics as a rule did not know much
about Renaissance and seventeenth-century thought and
feeling and in particular had a half-informed dislike of
Puritanism—of which, in point of fact, very little can be
found in Milton's poetry. Thus the critics were inclined
to blot out the "fundamentalist" poet-prophet in order to
save and glorify the sublime artist, the organ-voice. In
the first third of our own century some critics went on to
denigrate Milton the artist (or the man) as well.

Meanwhile, about 1917, American scholars had begun
the historical and interpretative process of recovering the
true and the whole Milton and the nature and background of his thought. That process has gone on steadily
to fuller and richer understanding. It can now be said
with assurance that modern enlightenment has brought
us much closer to the real Milton than earlier generations
ever got. The first step was the replacing of the old figure
of the grim Puritan by the Christian humanist of the
Renaissance whose all-embracing creed of liberty and
discipline was both radical and conservative. Then the
separation of the grand organ-voice from the beliefs and
ideas it uttered gave way to a unified conception of the
publicist and the poet, the Christian and the classicist,
whose "simple, sensuous, and passionate" art grew directly out of his deepest convictions and highest visions.

Finally, that art has been explored with a fresh aesthetic perceptiveness, grounded in sympathetic comprehension of Milton's ideas, which has made the reading of the poetry a more exciting and more authentic experience than traditional one-sided generalities could promote.

Widespread critical activity is not, to be sure, a guarantee of widespread interest among even literary readers; and contemporary poets seem to be aware of Milton only as people are aware of the Elgin Marbles. It is natural for readers to be drawn chiefly to the mirrors and interpreters of their own age and, in addition, to those select older writers whom current fashion has canonized—a group to which, as we observed at the start, Milton has not been admitted. But the most ardent champions of contemporary literature assume as a matter of course that it reflects a sick time, a time of public and private confusion, corruption, and violence, a time which at once craves and disowns ideals of direction and stability; and readers apparently absorb the endless presentations of such a world and recoil from writers who are not content to wallow in realism and despair. If we turn away from poetic greatness that is supposedly unapproachable, or from greatness that is bound up with religious and moral "heroism," we miss a large, central, and unique part of our poetic heritage. "Heritage," however, is perhaps not the right word, since Milton's vision of life and his bold and exalted art live rather beyond and above than behind us. In the noble judgment of Coleridge, "He was, as every truly great poet has ever been, a good man; but finding it impossible to realize his own aspirations, either in religion or politics, or society, he gave up his heart to the living spirit and light within him, and avenged himself on the world by enriching it with this record of his own transcendent ideal."

SUGGESTIONS FOR
FURTHER READING

The standard edition of Milton's complete works is that published by Columbia University (20 vols., 1931–1940). Among countless one-volume editions are *The Student's Milton*, ed. F. A. Patterson, which contains almost all the writings, the early biographies, and some apparatus, and *Complete Poems and Major Prose*, ed. M. Y. Hughes (1957), which has full introductions, notes, and references to scholarship and criticism. Some paperback editions of selected poems (most of them including selected prose) are those edited by D. Bush (1949), C. Brooks (1950), N. Frye (1951), E. Le Comte (1961), and M. H. Nicolson (1962); and J. T. Shawcross's *Complete English Poetry* (1963).

For biography there are: *Early Lives of Milton*, ed. H. Darbishire (1932); D. Masson's 7-volume *Life* (1859–1896), which, though out of date in some respects, is valuable for the resolute reader; J. H. Hanford, *John Milton, Englishman* (1949); J. M. French, *Life Records of John Milton* (5 vols., 1949–1958); and a biography forthcoming from W. R. Parker.

Some of the older critics, from Dryden onward,

were mentioned in the text. J. Thorpe's *Milton Criticism* (1950) is a handy anthology with modern emphasis; a similar collection is in prospect from the Oxford University Press. Hanford's *Milton Handbook* (4th ed., 1946) is a useful compendium of information and criticism. E. M. W. Tillyard's *Milton* (1930) was somewhat modified by his *Miltonic Setting* (1938) and *Studies in Milton* (1951). D. Daiches' *Milton* (1957) is a mainly critical survey. Marjorie Nicolson's *John Milton: A reader's guide to his poetry* (1963) is the harvest of many years of notable teaching and research. M. Y. Hughes and others are editing a large variorum commentary on all the poems.

Some discussions of the early poems are: J. H. Hanford, "The Youth of Milton," *Studies in Shakespeare, Milton and Donne* (1925); A. S. P. Woodhouse, on *Comus*, in the *University of Toronto Quarterly*, XI (1941–1942) and XIX (1949–1950); Rosemond Tuve, *Images and Themes in Five Poems by Milton* (1957); *Milton's Lycidas: The Tradition and the Poem* (1961), ed. C. A. Patrides, a collection of modern essays.

Books on *Paradise Lost* have been appearing lately at the rate of two or three a year. Some are: C. S. Lewis, *A Preface to Paradise Lost* (1942); Sir Maurice Bowra, *From Virgil to Milton* (1945); J. S. Diekhoff, *Paradise Lost: A Commentary on the Argument* (1946); B. Rajan, *Paradise Lost and the Seventeenth Century Reader* (1947); Arnold Stein, *Answerable Style* (1953); I. G. MacCaffrey, *Paradise Lost as "Myth"* (1959); J. H. Summers, *The Muse's Method* (1962); Anne D. Ferry, *Milton's Epic Voice* (1963); and Christopher Ricks, *Milton's Grand Style*

(1963). K. Svendsen's *Milton and Science* (1956) deals mainly with *Paradise Lost*.

Much recent writing on *Paradise Regained* is in periodicals. A. Stein has a full critique of it and *Samson* in *Heroic Knowledge* (1957). Two more special studies are E. M. Pope, *Paradise Regained: The Tradition and the Poem* (1947), and W. R. Parker, *Milton's Debt to Greek Tragedy in Samson Agonistes* (1937).

Milton's complete prose works are being edited in 8 volumes, with very elaborate commentaries, by D. M. Wolfe and others (vols. I, II, III, 1953, 1959, 1962). The fullest single interpretation is Arthur Barker's *Milton and the Puritan Dilemma* (1942). M. Kelley's *This Great Argument* (1941) deals with the theology of the *Christian Doctrine* and *Paradise Lost*. Milton is prominent in W. Haller's *The Rise of Puritanism* (1938) and *Liberty and Reformation in the Puritan Revolution* (1955). The standard history of the period is Godfrey Davies's *The Early Stuarts 1603–1660* (1937; rev. 1959).

Bibliographies by D. H. Stevens (1930) and C. Huckabay (1960) cover Miltoniana from 1800 to 1957. There are ample lists in the *Cambridge Bibliography of English Literature*, ed. F. W. Bateson (4 vols., 1940), and its *Supplement*, ed. G. Watson (1957), and in D. Bush, *English Literature in the Earlier Seventeenth Century* (rev. ed., 1962).

INDEX